"Bryan and Brittany have managed to capture their drive to serve clients by blending mindset and money. Having known Bryan and Brittany for more than two decades, one thing holds true: their desire to impact not only their clients' lives but also the industry as a whole."

—**BRIAN HECKERT**, financial advisor and Founder of FSM Wealth

"I have had the privilege of working with hundreds of very successful, elite financial advisors. And in that time, I have never found a firm as committed to helping their clients achieve what is truly possible with their retirement dreams as I have in working with Sweet Financial."

—**CHRIS SMITH**, Creator of The Campfire Effect

DREAM
ARCHITECTURE

BUILD A RETIREMENT
BEYOND WHAT'S POSSIBLE

BRITTANY ANDERSON
and BRYAN J. SWEET

HOUNDSTOOTH
PRESS

DREAM ARCHITECTURE
Build a Retirement Beyond What's Possible

ISBN   978-1-5445-3087-1   *Hardcover*
　　　 978-1-5445-3088-8   *Paperback*
　　　 978-1-5445-3089-5   *Ebook*

CONTENTS

DISCLAIMER

This book does not purport to be a complete description of the securities, markets, or developments referred to in this material. Nothing in this book constitutes investment advice, performance data, or any recommendation that any particular security, portfolio of securities, transaction, or investment strategy is suitable for any specific person. Any mention of a specific security or strategy is not a recommendation to purchase such security or utilize such strategy. Sweet Financial Partners, LLC, manages client accounts using a variety of investment techniques and strategies, which are not necessarily discussed in this book. The information contained in this book has been obtained from sources considered to be reliable, but we do not guarantee that the foregoing material is accurate or complete. Any information is not a complete summary or statement of all available data necessary for making an investment decision. Any opinions, viewpoints, and analyses on the part of the chapter authors are those of the chapter authors and not necessarily those of Sweet Financial Partners, LLC. Expressions of opinion are as of the initial book publishing date and are subject to change without notice. Sweet Financial Partners is not responsible for the consequences of any particular transaction or investment decision based on the content of this book. All financial, retirement, and estate planning should be individualized, as each person's situation is unique. This information is not intended as a solicitation or an offer to buy or sell any security referred to herein. Keep in mind that there is no assurance that any recommendations or strategies will ultimately be successful, profitable, or protective against a loss. There may also be the potential for missed growth opportunities that may occur after the sale of an investment. Recommendations, specific investments, or strategies discussed may not be suitable for all investors. Past performance may not be indicative of future results. You should discuss any tax or legal matters with the appropriate professional.

This book is dedicated to our amazing team members at Sweet Financial who help our clients realize all that is possible every day. Without their dedication, focus on excellence, and commitment to serving our clients in the highest capacity, none of what we talk about in this book would be possible. We have cultivated a team that truly cares about our clients and each other, and for that we are forever grateful. The ability to deliver The Dream Architect™ experience to clients across the country has allowed us to take part in some amazing exchanges with people we are so grateful to serve. Our team brings The Dream Architect™ to life and helps make dreams become a reality for so many.

CHAPTER 1

POSSIBILITY COMES TO THOSE WHO CREATE IT

"Every possibility begins with
the courage to imagine."
—MARY ANNE RADMACHER

This book isn't for everyone.

If you want to think bigger than you've ever imagined and dream bigger dreams than you ever thought possible, we want to help you do that. But if you are okay with the status quo and aren't interested in realizing just how much is possible, then this book probably isn't for you. We understand that when it comes to planning for the future, some people don't want to talk about dreaming or possibilities.

However, if you want to pursue what sets your soul on fire, we can help you with that!

THIS BOOK IS THE PREQUEL TO OUR FIRST BOOK, *DARE TO DREAM*

In 2016, we published our first book, *Dare to Dream: Design the Retirement You Can't Wait to Wake Up To.* The book's goal is to explain how to gain clarity about and live according to your why in retirement, evaluate the health of your wealth, and safeguard your future. The book focuses on planning for the *distribution* phase of retirement—the phase in which you begin to live on the savings you gathered during your *accumulation* phase, which was the years of your life that you spent saving.

After we published the book, we realized it was missing essential information. In our daily work with clients, we constantly witness how critical a positive mindset is for embracing the *possibilities* that proper planning can create. As we walked our clients through our Dream Architect™ process, we began to see how critical a positive mindset is in people's ability to think, dream, and live even bigger lives than they know are possible.

This book is really the prequel to *Dare to Dream*. We believe your mindset and attitude have to be poised for possibility before you can optimize the process of planning for retirement.

We believe every person has the right to realize that their dreams are possible. Possibility comes to those who create it; it doesn't just appear mysteriously. In this book, we hope to help you define what *possibility* means to you.

WHY DO PEOPLE TEND TO THINK SMALL?

We see many adults getting stuck in a narrow vision of what their lives could really be like. They err on the side of caution and discretion, possibly at the expense of their ability to have an amazing future.

Many times, people are afraid to say out loud what they really want out of life. They think the people in their lives might look at them like they've lost their minds. Or they fear the repercussions if they make a bold statement about the future and then are unable to realize that dream. They tell themselves, "What if I don't really accomplish it? Then I will look stupid." And many times, a limited view of the possibilities simply comes from self-doubt.

We want to help people realize that self-doubt should not exist.

OUR DREAM ARCHITECT™ PROCESS BLENDS YOUR FINANCES WITH YOUR DREAMS

This is exactly why we created The Dream Architect™ process: we want to be the champions in people's corners. We want to be the people you can come to and say, "Here's what I want to accomplish" so we can be your most enthusiastic cheerleaders. This process blends your financial life with your dreams to create the retirement you can't wait to wake up to.

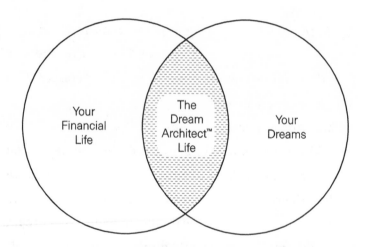

We understand that you're the sole architect of your dreams. Our mission isn't just to help manage your investments; it's to inspire you to pursue your biggest dreams *and help you get there.* Our proprietary process, The Dream

Architect™, is a four-step approach to inspire, create, build, and execute a plan that's in alignment with your goals and vision for the future.

Step in The Dream Architect™ Process	What We Accomplish in This Step
1. Vision	Where are you now, and where would you like to be? During a complimentary Discovery Call, you'll share your financial foundation, what's most important to you, and the future you envision for yourself, your family, and your legacy. Afterward, we'll meet and explore how our team can support you on your journey.
2. Blueprint	To build dreams, a Dream Architect™ must first have a blueprint of what matters most and why. During this step, we attempt to dig even deeper to discover the true motivation beneath your biggest goals. We'll conduct a risk assessment on your portfolio and run it through different market scenarios. Although these results won't guarantee success, they will help us determine if your plan has the ability to withstand potential obstacles. From there, we'll recommend improvements with your dreams and goals at the forefront.

3. Build	With a deep knowledge of your vision and a blueprint, it's time to build. We'll construct your customized plan that includes a critical component for success—an implementation schedule. Because your goals and dreams are unique to you, each build is tailored to your values and vision of the future. This creates a plan to live by *every. Single. Day.*
4. Maintenance	This is the most important step to ensure your plan is being executed properly over time. We'll meet with you one to three times a year to share updates, revise your customized blueprint (if necessary), and ensure it remains aligned as your goals, dreams, and financial situation evolve. Although we'll have a regular review schedule, we are here for you anytime, especially during life's biggest transitions.

ONCE YOUR GOALS ARE IN FOCUS, IT IS EASIER FOR THEM TO MANIFEST

We believe it is important to clarify and write down your dreams and goals. Once you put what you really want out into the universe, it can't help but transpire to make it happen. This is the basic premise of a "New Thought" principle called the Law of Attraction: the ability to attract into our lives whatever we focus on. The Law of Attraction uses the power of the mind to materialize our thoughts into reality. The Law of Attraction website says, "If you focus on negative doom and gloom, you will remain under that cloud. If you focus on positive thoughts and have goals that you aim to achieve, you will find a way to achieve them with massive action."[1]

We can give you many examples of how the Law of Attraction has worked for us—from new opportunities and new relationships to accomplishing some of our biggest goals we didn't think were possible. These personal experiences flowed from simply focusing on what we wanted and taking action toward those desires. What you think, believe, and focus on will manifest in your life. But if you keep your dreams inside and don't verbalize them or focus on them, they are not likely to happen.

THINK LIKE A KID

Have you ever noticed how creative kids are? They think big, without constraints. If you ask a kid a question, their

---

[1] "What Is the Law of Attraction? Open Your Eyes to a World of Endless Possibilities," TheLawofAttraction.com, accessed February 7, 2022, https://www.thelawofattraction.com/what-is-the-law-of-attraction.

imagination will run wild and come up with answers you would probably never think of. But once we become adults, we seem to lose that great imagination. The older people get, the narrower their focus tends to become. They find their minds squeezed into a small box.

Sometimes we limit our view of what's possible because of social pressures—we don't want our friends and colleagues to tell us we're "thinking too big." This isn't just our observation; it's something that science has documented.

In a longitudinal test of creative potential, a NASA study found that 98 percent of 1,600 four- and five-year-olds scored at a "creative genius" level. Five years later, only 30 percent of the same group of children scored at the same level, and again, five years later, only 12 percent. When the same test was administered to adults, it was found that only 2 percent scored at this genius level.[2]

So what changes? Why do we become less creative as we become adults?

According to the NASA study, education drains our creativity. As we learn to excel at *convergent* thinking—the

2   Rohini Venkatraman, "You're 96 Percent Less Creative than You Were as a Child. Here's How to Reverse That," *Inc.*, January 18, 2018, https://www.inc.com/rohini-venkatraman/4-ways-to-get-back-creativity-you-had-as-a-kid.html.

ability to focus, make decisions, criticize, and evaluate—we quash our instinct for *divergence*, or imagination, which we use to generate new possibilities.

Dr. George Land, a general systems scientist, gave a TEDx Tucson presentation titled "The Failure of Success" in 2011. He said, "Divergent thinking works like an accelerator, and convergent thinking puts a brake on our best efforts. When we look inside the brain, we find that neurons are fighting each other and actually diminishing the power of the brain, because we're constantly judging, criticizing, and censoring." To think more creatively, he suggested we quit doing that.[3]

HOW TO REIGNITE YOUR CREATIVITY

The good news is, we can summon the creative genius in our five-year-old selves again with a little effort. One way to do so is simply to listen to positive, uplifting music.

In 2017, a team of researchers found that creativity was higher in participants who listened to "happy music" (e.g., classical music high on arousal and positive mood) while performing a divergent creativity task than it was in

---

3   George Land, "The Failure of Success," YouTube video, 13:06, https://www.youtube.com/watch?v=ZfKMq-rYtnc.

participants who performed the task in silence. (No effect of music was found for convergent thinking.)[4]

In a *Psychology Today* article, Fran Sorin, a coach, author, and inspirational speaker, says that teaching yourself to see what is possible rather than what isn't possible is the hallmark of imagination. (See why we love the concept of "possibilities" so much?)

When you're tasked with doing something new and unfamiliar, Sorin says, "rather than heading down the path of impossibility, which closes your neural pathway, take the other path of opening to possibility (even if you experience self-doubt), knowing that there is always more than one solution to a problem and that you're going to figure it out."[5]

A second suggestion Sorin has for jump-starting your creative thinking process is to spend some time in nature. She says, "Take a daily nature walk with the sole purpose of being in and connecting with nature. No friends, children,

---

4   Simone M. Ritter and Sam Ferguson, "Happy Creativity: Listening to Happy Music Facilitates Divergent Thinking," *PLOS ONE* 12, no. 9 (2017): e0182210, https://journals.plos.org/plosone/article?id=10.1371/journal.pone.0182210.

5   Fran Sorin, "7 Simple Yet Effective Ways to Jump-Start Your Imagination," *Psychology Today*, February 1, 2017, https://www.psychologytoday.com/us/blog/tools-innovative-living/201702/7-simple-yet-effective-ways-jump-start-your-imagination.

or technology allowed. Even if you spend ten minutes a day doing this, you'll be surprised at how it ignites your imagination and creativity."[6]

Speaking with others is another way we have found to ignite your imagination if you're feeling stuck in a rut. Talking through your project and its process with someone who isn't involved can reignite your creativity; for example, that person might suggest things you haven't considered. For true creative genius, talk with a child and watch their mind take off, unhindered by fear of what others might think or by preconceived ideas.

We want you to think like a kid again, to think in terms of optimum possibilities. In addition to determining what elements go into an individual's retirement plan, we see an important part of our role as encouraging and guiding people to go far beyond their usual thought process. We want to help them see that there is so much possibility in their future and that even after going through major life transitions, they will still be okay.

We want to help people become aware of the limiting way they may be thinking about the future. We hope this book helps increase that awareness.

---

6   Sorin, "7 Simple Yet Effective Ways."

LET PASSION AND PURPOSE OVERCOME FEAR

We see people work hard their entire lives, saving their money and planning for the moment when they are ready to step into retirement. But somewhere along the way, they lose sight of what's possible. Even people who have an extremely comfortable cushion saved up still worry "Will I have enough?" In essence, *fear* is leading them to ask this question.

We want you to look forward to retirement with passion and purpose instead of second-guessing yourself during that journey because of fear-based assumptions. When you discover all the ways we can help you put your money to work for you, you'll start to see the possibilities.

Another limiting mindset we have seen among many of our clients is that they think they have to wait until they retire to begin pursuing the lives they want. We want you to identify and begin pursuing your dreams now! Then, once you get to retirement, you likely will have even more freedom to continue and expand the activities you enjoy, further pursuing your passion and purpose.

So what is a dream anyway? In our first book, we defined it like this:

A *dream* is a pleasurable vision of what the future can become that fills you with energy, speaks to your heart, and strengthens your will and ability to overcome all roadblocks to achieve it.[7]

Having engaged in hundreds of "discovery" conversations with clients, there have been times when we almost had to pry their dreams out of them. That limited imagination rears its ugly head time and again. When we ask what people really want to do in retirement, they say things like, "Maybe I'll take one big vacation" or "I would like to get a new car." It can be hard to see the forest for the trees, and some people don't realize they are limiting their vision of the future. We enjoy the process of expanding their awareness about what is possible.

We want you to have a clear vision of a future brimming with fulfillment, satisfaction, and joy. But unless you know what direction you're trying to go, you'll wind up in an arbitrary traffic lane to an unknown destination.

DIGGING DEEPER TO DISCOVER THE MEANING BEHIND THE TANGIBLE PURCHASE

As we work with clients, we strive to go beyond face-value answers. Instead, we want to dig deeper to get to the core

---

7   Bryan Sweet, *Dare to Dream: Design the Retirement You Can't Wait to Wake Up To* (Scotts Valley, CA: CreateSpace, 2016), 77.

of *why* someone is choosing a certain goal. We will ask someone a question, and when they provide the answer, we'll ask *why* it's the answer. We continue doing so until we get to the essence of *why* the person wants what they want—the true meaning of that thing or event.

Many financial advisors have some version of the following conversation with their clients:

"What do you wish for in your retirement?"

"I really want to buy a brand-new vehicle."

"Okay, great. Let's start planning for that. How much do you think you would spend on that?"

In our view, that bare-bones approach fails to get to the heart of why that person wants a new vehicle. We prefer to go much deeper.

If a client tells us "I want to buy a new vehicle," we will ask, "Okay, which vehicle? Which one do you have your eye on?"

The client might say, "My wife and I have always had practical vehicles because we had kids. But now that they are grown, I want something a little bit less practical. I would love to buy a sporty car."

One of our advisors might say, "Talk to us about that. Why do you want a sporty vehicle?"

He might say, "I've wanted a red convertible ever since I was a kid."

"Wow, that's interesting. Tell me about that. How did that feel, being a kid, looking forward to getting your license and picturing yourself in that shiny red convertible?"

The client might say, "Oh, it was so much fun! I used to talk to my brother about it."

We probe further by saying something like, "Wow! Does your brother know you're looking at that dream car? I'll bet a road trip is in your future!"

And the client responds with, "My brother passed away this last year."

It's amazing how many times these heart-stopping moments come about just because we refuse to accept a surface answer. Now we know we are connecting and able to go deeper. We know we're getting somewhere, and we ask the client to talk more about his brother. Soon, we find out that this client wants to buy a red convertible because he is honoring his memory of his brother, a pact they made as siblings, decades earlier. So, really, the tangible item—the car—isn't the heart of this client's dream. What matters to him is the story behind it. It is essential that we uncover the true meaning behind each individual's dreams.

The true meaning behind a person's dream runs deep. That's why we take the time to dig through those layers.

We want to discover what drives people. When we discover their true why, we can help them build a future with meaning. The car doesn't matter. The vacation home doesn't matter. The RV and boat don't matter. What matters is the why—the meaning and purpose behind those tangible purchases that will make a difference in their lives.

POSSIBILITIES INSPIRE US TO OVERCOME BARRIERS

We have found that the concept of *possibility* can be incredibly inspiring and empowering to people facing difficult transitions.

However, while we plan for and dream about the future, unexpected scenarios can arise and complicate our journey. Getting sick or injured, losing a business or loved one, getting divorced—none of these scenarios are a part of anyone's plan. When people encounter frustrating and sometimes devastating transitions in life, we want them to realize that there is still a world of exciting possibilities on the other side of that situation.

Possibility becomes even more important when you are navigating a difficult or traumatic situation. Focusing on possibilities can help you maintain the positive mindset you need to get through the ordeal so you can still show up for yourself and your loved ones.

In the real world, we often face uncertainty and difficulty. We are writing this book in the middle of the COVID-
19 pandemic. No one saw this challenge coming, and the
upheaval it has caused has been difficult for some, devastating for others. The pandemic has strained millions of
people's finances, relationships, and health. We want to
help you navigate those storms and discover how you can
prevail and thrive despite any setbacks.

A big part of that process is maintaining a sense of hope
and optimism. Always look for the light at the end of the
tunnel, and don't let the situation rob you of your dreams.
Reach out to the people around you who will be happy to
support, encourage, and help you.

Spend time with positive people. You might be surprised at how much they inspire you to identify your
dreams and go after them.

We had a mentor, Sean Clinch Stephenson, who was born
with an extremely rare condition called osteogenesis imper-
fecta. The condition prevented Sean's bones from growing
normally, and as a consequence, they were extremely brit-
tle. Although he never grew past three feet, many people
called him "the three-foot giant" for good reason.

Sean did not allow his condition to hinder the opportunity
he saw for his future. He was a successful self-help author,
therapist, and public speaker. His inspirational videos had

millions of views on YouTube. Doctors had not expected him to live into adulthood. By the time he was eighteen years old, he had suffered more than two hundred fractures in all parts of his body. But he found strength despite his disability, and by the time he was seventeen, he was already giving motivational speeches. He graduated from DePaul University with a bachelor's degree in political science in 2001. Afterward, he worked as an intern for President Bill Clinton and Congressman Bill Lipinski of Illinois.[8]

Unfortunately, the world lost a great man when Sean passed away in the summer of 2019, at the age of forty, after a fall that resulted in a head injury.[9] Even though Sean endured massive amounts of pain and was in and out of consciousness, moments before he passed, it became even more evident how truly special he was. Through his pain and suffering, he gained a moment of clarity, sat up, and said, "This is happening *for* me, not *to* me."[10]

---

8   Sweet and Anderson, *Dare to Dream*, 77.
9   John T. Didymus, "Sean Stephenson Death: Author and Therapist Dies due to Complications after Suffering a Head Injury," *Monsters & Critics*, August 30, 2019, https://www.monstersandcritics.com/celebrity/sean-stephenson-death-author-and-therapist-dies-due-to-complications-after-suffering-head-injury.
10 The Gratitude Podcast, "In Loving Memory of Sean Stephenson, the 3ft Giant—How to Choose Gratitude When Life Seems Unfair," YouTube video, 31:31, August 29, 2019, https://www.youtube.com/watch?v=Q1YYBIwH8eU.

Wouldn't it make it so much easier to overcome life's obstacles if we had the positive mindset that Sean had? We can all aspire to that. We all face hardships, but the ones who come out on top realize, like Sean did: "Yes, that happened, but I have to find purpose in this situation. I have to find a way that serves me instead of letting it hold me back."

When everything around us seems to be going wrong, such as during the pandemic, it is important to stay focused on our dreams and on possibilities. Don't let the negative environment feed your self-doubt. If necessary, stop watching the news.

When you listen to bad news long enough, pretty soon your brain assumes it's reality and then you start living that reality. This idea is demonstrated through the Baader-Meinhof phenomenon of frequency bias: when you experience something that is new to you—be it a new car, a new trip you want to take, or a new house design—suddenly, you see it everywhere. In a study on *Healthline* that referenced the Baader-Meinhof phenomenon, the writer states, "In reality, there is no unusual frequency in occurrence. It's just that you've started to notice it."[11]

---

11   Ann Pietrangelo, "What the Baader-Meinhof Phenomenon Is and Why You May See It Again...and Again," *Healthline*, last modified December 17, 2019, https://www.healthline.com/health/baader-meinhof-phenomenon#what-it-is.

Be conscious of what you allow to enter your ears and eyes. Avoid anything that will keep you from living your purpose and passion. Put up a barrier against those discouragements, and ask yourself if what you are about to hear and see motivates you to move toward your greater vision for your life. If the answer is no, then it's time to redirect your attention. Otherwise, it could be difficult to overcome the negativity coming at you from all directions.

Do whatever it takes to stay positive and focus on your best imaginable future.

BUSINESS OWNERS, SEEK YOUR IDENTITY BEYOND YOUR WORK

Business owners who are planning for retirement have unique situations and challenges. A person's entire identity is often wrapped up in the business that they have nurtured for decades.

If you are a business owner, we want you to think in terms of your optimum possibility—beyond the work so familiar to you. What does life look like after selling your business or bringing in a successor? How can you ensure that your business carries on? What is your exit strategy? What is the legacy you want to leave?

Sometimes when you're knee deep in the day-to-day operations, it can be difficult to see possibility on the other side. You've been caught up in the whirlwind for so long and you're so close to the minutiae that it can be difficult to see beyond your role as a business owner.

We understand that possibility looks different to everybody. At Sweet Financial Partners, we can help you find that possibility. What we mean by discovering possibility is that we can help you confidently answer the question "What's next?"

Your business has been your "baby" for decades, and it has been successful. But what comes next? Sometimes the answer requires reinventing ourselves, even when we are not ready to retire.

Danny Meyer, a highly successful restaurateur who owned the Michelin-starred Gramercy Tavern and nineteen other top-rated restaurants in New York City, had to lay off nearly 2,100 people in mid-March 2020. He kept a core group of seventy employees to keep the Union Square Hospitality Group—the company he spent thirty-five years building—in operation. His business went from more than $100 million in revenue in 2019 to zero overnight.

But instead of crumbling under the weight of that significant loss, Meyer views this unprecedented shift as a wake-up call. He believes that "the COVID crisis has exposed an ugly truth: that the restaurant industry is broken, and now is the time to rethink not only how to social distance restaurant kitchens, but everything about the business model, from employee pay and tipping, to impossibly high rents." He has in his mind a vision of what the future of the hospitality industry will look like. "I see restaurant dining rooms that are staffed by a much more diverse group of people," he says. "I see restaurants that love you more than they ever did. I see a lot less attitude at front doors, a lot less small talk around the table...I see authenticity."[12]

Meyer tried to reinvent what his restaurant looked when public health orders shut down in-room dining. It would have been easy for Meyer to view this situation as a negative, but instead, he considered possibilities—what his business could look like on the other side of the pandemic—and he stayed optimistic. We're guessing that he will build an enterprise that is even more successful than what he had before.

The ability to stay optimistic during times of uncertainty and upheaval is an incredible skill, and most people

---

12   Jay Kernis, "Danny Meyer on the Key Takeaway for Rescuing Restaurants," CBS News, July 26, 2020, https://www.cbsnews.com/news/danny-meyer-on-the-key-takeaway-for-rescuing-restaurants.

don't possess it. Many people would give up at that point, and then the future could look pretty grim. But when you get creative and think outside the box, then great results can develop. Ask yourself, *What else can I do?* and *How can I do this differently?* In the end, our new creations are often much better than what we were doing before. It sometimes takes a difficult situation to get you to the next level.

When you are open to possibilities, amazing things can happen.

We saw a quote recently from an unknown source that states, "Sometimes life doesn't give you what you think you want—not because you don't deserve it, but because you deserve more." We agree 100 percent. Sometimes we plan for what we expect to happen in the future, but then a situation blindsides us. Being battered by external forces we can do nothing about feels like a punch to the gut, but we must always be willing to think beyond what we had originally pictured for the future, which might not be possible anymore. The great news is, though, that sometimes the unexpected situation can prompt us to take our efforts in an entirely different and better direction—one we would have never considered if we hadn't been forced out of our comfort zone.

Nothing is guaranteed. Sometimes life has a funny way of changing your plans for you. So how do you prepare in the best way possible? It's like life has kicked out one leg of your chair; you still want the other three legs to be able to support you.

REDISCOVER YOUR PERSONAL VALUE SYSTEM

When unexpected circumstances make it impossible for us to continue doing business as usual, we need to rediscover our personal value system.

Many times, when we work with business owners, we see that they have a blurred line between their business value system and personal value system. Business owners often get so caught up in their businesses that they have forgotten who they are outside their identity as business owners.

It is important to ask yourself, "What do I value most in life? What is important to me now, outside this business?" We have seen business owners who were so driven to achieve success that when they no longer had their business, they almost had to reteach themselves how to be fully present for their families.

We work with business owners to clarify their personal values so that whatever decisions they make are aligned with their personal values. That's why we dig deep to get to the core, the heart of what they value most, and then help them build up from that foundation. When you make decisions based on your top three core values, you are more likely to end up in a great spot.

YOUR POSSIBILITIES TOOLBOX

1. **Build a dream board.** Once you begin to identify the true meaning behind your dreams for the future, we can help you visualize the various elements of those dreams. We will work with you to create a dream board—a bulletin board filled with photos and other representations of your dreams—that will serve as a visual reminder of those things. Your dream board will continue to inspire you and help you feel excitement about your retirement journey. One of our clients takes their dream board with them when they travel. Both husband and wife have sent us photos from their trips that relate to the dreams they are working toward. It is incredibly inspiring, both for them and for us.

2. **Ask yourself, What if?** Imagine that life, or work, as you know it right now were to change suddenly in a drastic way. What could you do differently? How could this unexpected situation actually improve your outcome? Think big! Think like a kid, with no boundaries to your imagination!

3. **Access our Retirement Readiness Center** at *www.mysweetfinancial.com* to get started on dreaming! Spend some extra time on the Visioning tool that helps you create a visual of what retirement might look like.

CHAPTER 2

DECIDE WHAT YOU WANT

"You can't go back and change the
beginning, but you can start where
you are and change the ending."

—C. S. LEWIS

Some say *expectation* is the root of all heartache.
We believe *indecision* is the root of all heartache.
Sometimes our biggest stress comes from inde-
cisions, big and small.

OVERCOME DECISION FATIGUE

*"It's not hard to make decisions when
you know what your values are."*

—Roy Disney

What we mean by that is that many times, some of our biggest stressors come from knowing you have big decisions to make for your future, or for the present, yet you are unable to do so. Often, this inaction is caused by a thing called *decision fatigue*.

Decision fatigue can happen in every aspect of our lives—even in our everyday routines. For example, maybe you've worked hard all day long and juggled meetings and deadlines, plus kids, traffic, and errands. You get home at the end of the day and ask your spouse, "What should we have for dinner?"

You and your spouse just stare at each other, both thinking, "I don't know. I can't make another decision." One simple question has turned into one of the most difficult to answer because you've made so many decisions all day long. You simply cannot fathom making another one.

An article in *The New York Times* explains this phenomenon: "Decision fatigue helps explain why ordinarily sensible people get angry at colleagues and families, splurge on clothes, buy junk food at the supermarket, and can't resist the dealer's offer to rustproof their new car. No matter how rational and high-minded you try to be, you can't make decision after decision without paying a biological price."[13]

Knowing what you want takes a lot of anxiety out of the decision-making process. We believe that if you know what you want most in life, it will make all your other decisions easier. And that alone can help prevent decision fatigue.

Not only does indecision keep you stuck in life, incapable of moving forward; it can also make you feel like you are not in control of your own path in life. We believe decisiveness is synonymous with control.

YOUR IDEAL RETIREMENT

When we begin talking to people about retirement, most of them focus on what they are retiring *from* instead of what they are retiring *to*. For example, they look forward to retiring *from* the drudgery of a job they dislike or *from* the constant pressure to perform well and compete for a slice of the corporate pie.

---

13   John Tierney, "Do You Suffer from Decision Fatigue?" *The New York Times*, August 17, 2011, https://www.nytimes.com/2011/08/21/magazine/do-you-suffer-from-decision-fatigue.html.

We encourage you to spend more time thinking about what you are retiring *to*—maybe you will retire *to* a life of service or *to* spending time in another part of the world.

We talked a lot about this concept in our first book, *Dare to Dream: Design the Retirement You Can't Wait to Wake Up To*. Here's an excerpt:

> **"What am I retiring from, and what am I retiring to?"** This is the *single most important question* you can ask yourself as you discover what your future should look like. Maybe you shouldn't retire yet. Or at all. Or maybe you should be doing a different type of work than you're doing now. Would it be more fulfilling for you to do something rewarding that pays less? We want you to get the most out of your retirement and fill your days with all the things you love. To accomplish that, again, you need to know what your personal why is. Maybe you are retiring from a structured schedule in the manufacturing business, and now you are retiring to a more relaxed schedule that includes spending time with your grandkids, developing your hobbies, and working part time in a job you're passionate about. Do you have a dream of living in Florida, but you've never even visited there? Test it out! Do you want to take up a hobby like hiking, knitting, or painting, but you've never tried it?

Test all of your dreams out to see if they live up to the way you are envisioning them.[14]

If you don't make a decision about what your ideal life looks like, it's going to be hard for *any* wealth advisor to put your money to work for you. And isn't that the point of saving? To take that hard-earned money and have it support your ideal future?

It's critical to make wise, *informed* decisions leading up to retirement. We recommend working with a competent, knowledgeable financial advisor who helps people retire every day. It can be overwhelming to make all those important decisions about your future by yourself. You face decisions about how to save, how your money will be distributed, and what the heck you'll do with your time. Many times, when people try to navigate this journey alone, they freeze and don't do anything.

Indecision and inaction can cause problems for the future. If you don't have anything to aim for in retirement, you're like an arrow without a target—you may be able to launch forward, but what you'll hit is completely unknown. It is important to decide what you want and then take the necessary steps to achieve that dream.

---

14   Sweet and Anderson, *Dare to Dream*, 25–26.

You've spent all these years working hard and saving diligently. All the effort you've put in throughout your entire life basically leads up to this point. You don't want indecision to be the cause of you not moving forward in a positive and productive way and robbing you of the ability to see the possibility that's ahead of you. That is exactly why we designed our proprietary process called The Dream Architect™ to address this critical rite of passage.

We recently saw a quote by an unknown author that captures the importance of knowing what you want as early in life as possible so you can enjoy the journey:

> Retirement age is sixty-seven. Life expectancy is seventy-eight. Work for fifty years to enjoy maybe eleven? Start enjoying life now. No one is guaranteed tomorrow.

Don't wait until "later" or "someday" to decide what you want most. Not only will a clear goal help you have a more fulfilled life; it also can help you build wealth in a different way, with more purpose and passion. As you work hard every day, you will constantly be aware of the dream you're aiming to fulfill. Doesn't that sound more exciting than marking the days off the calendar in a countdown to the day when you don't have to go to work anymore?

THE MOST IMPORTANT DECISION TO MAKE

"The two most important days in your life are the day you are born and the day you find out why."
—Mark Twain

We believe the most important decision you need to make is in response to this question: what do you want most in this life? Once you know why you are here—what your purpose is in life—we believe that all other decisions become so much easier.

Next, you need to surround yourself with positive, uplifting people who can push you to be that best version of yourself. Having the right mindset serves as the backdrop to every decision we make. It is absolutely critical to have a positive mindset focused on possibilities and then clearly articulate what you want out of this life, regardless of the stage you're in. Sometimes, again, it's difficult to do so by ourselves. It helps to surround yourself with positive people who dream big and who believe in you. Whether it's your spouse, a friend, a family member, or your financial advisor, find an accountability partner who will work with you to defeat self-limiting beliefs, rewrite your story, and figure out what you really want in this one life we're given.

If you aren't clear about what you want, you won't know where you are headed or how to get to your ideal future. It can be difficult to put a plan in place unless you know what you are striving for. Clarity around your biggest dreams for your future is critical, especially when you are facing major life events and navigating significant transitions.

MAKING DECISIONS DURING MAJOR LIFE TRANSITIONS

Gaining clarity about where you're headed not only makes every decision easier; it also serves as a roadmap to follow during major life transitions.

For example, if your spouse were to die unexpectedly in an accident, and if you had never sat down and made decisions about your finances and your future, how would you feel? Suddenly, you're grieving and mourning the loss of your life partner, while also having to make large, impactful decisions around your finances. Making those decisions is difficult enough on a good day.

Decide what you want as early as possible, with your significant other, when you are in good health and not in the throes of a life-altering situation. You will be so grateful that you took the time now to work through the "tough stuff," rather than waiting for the someday that could come too late.

When people decide what they want and make their wishes known in writing, it allows their loved ones to honor their wishes once they pass away.

Before Bryan's aunt Jean died, she said she wanted yellow roses at her funeral. It might sound like a small detail, but because we knew what she wanted, we were able to honor her by fulfilling her wish. Knowing what she wanted was a gift to us.

If you have been prone to inaction all your life, it can take some practice to become decisive. Start small, and know that you don't have to figure everything out right this second. What matters is that you're making progress toward the big question that needs answering—what you want most out of this life. We get only one shot.

REPLACE THE SELF-LIMITING BELIEFS THAT LEAD TO INDECISION

Darren Hardy, a success mentor to CEOs and high achievers, says the greatest inhibitor to our potential success is self-limiting beliefs, which prevent us from stepping up and into our greater potential and living our best lives. One self-limiting emotional state, Hardy says, is hopelessness, in which we say to ourselves, "This won't happen for me; things like that happen for other people." Seeing an opportunity isn't enough; you must *believe* you can achieve it. Hopelessness comes when we allow negativity to pervade our consciousness and to rob us of our ability to dream big. To combat hopelessness, Hardy says, "immerse yourself in a new belief system of success, full of positivity and hope." He recommends bombarding your consciousness with positive beliefs from what you read, listen to, and watch, as well as from the people you hang out with.[15]

So how do these self-limiting beliefs become powerful, invading our thoughts and causing us to miss out on valuable possibilities? Many of them formed when we were children, when people told us things we believed but weren't necessarily true. We internalized those stories as the truth and never reexamined them.

Psychiatrist and Harvard Medical School professor John Sharp said in a 2019 TEDx Talk that a self-limiting belief is "the story you've been telling yourself about who you are and how everything always plays out." He adds, "The worst part about the false truth...is that it becomes

---

15   "Daily Mentoring with Darren Hardy," Facebook video, 3:16, March 21, 2016,
      https://www.facebook.com/DarrenHardyFan/videos/10154066872107287.

our self-fulfilling prophecy, the basis of what we expect from ourselves in the future." And he says that our inaccurate narratives are what we default to when we're faced with difficulty or disappointment.[16]

To overcome these damaging beliefs, Sharp recommends that we simply rewrite our stories. First, we need to do some soul searching to identify where our narrative diverges from reality. If we find ourselves thinking, *I always struggle with making decisions, I'm always quick to react,* or *I never get what I want,* it's a good indication that we are reciting a narrative from long ago that no longer serves us. He suggests replacing these statements with positive statements about yourself.

Start by flipping the negative narrative in your head:

- Instead of believing *I always struggle with making decisions*, believe *I am a decisive person.*
- Instead of believing *I'm always quick to react*, believe *I am a patient person.*
- Instead of believing *I never get what I want*, believe *I always have what I need.*

---

16 Mary Halton, "What Old Story about Yourself Are You Still Believing? Here's How to Find It and Change It," Ted.com, January 24, 2019, https://ideas.ted.com/what-old-story-about-yourself-are-you-still-believing-heres-how-to-find-it-and-change-it.

The point here is that to grow as human beings, we must push ourselves to think new thoughts and see ourselves in a new light. Positive growth and change will not happen if we maintain limiting thought patterns and beliefs.

MAKING A DECISION IS A POWERFUL ACTION

Once you decide what you want and make an outward commitment to get it—"I'm deciding to go after X" or "I'm deciding to pursue Y"—our opinion is that the universe can't help but conspire with you to help you achieve that goal. Again, we believe that whatever you focus on will manifest in your life.

Now, we want to start by saying that this section of the chapter is not all woo-woo or just fluff stuff. Rather, it is based on our experiences and the amazing opportunities we've had in walking alongside so many on their path to getting the most out of life.

Once you are clear about what you want and you tell other people about your dream, they can support you and help you move toward that goal. Your chance of success becomes exponentially higher because you have the people around you telling you that you can do it versus people telling you, "Oh, that's off the wall," or "How on earth is that going to happen?" or "That's probably not possible." This is why it's important to surround yourself with people who are rooting for you and want you to succeed.

What's more, once people start seeing the energy your clear vision gives you and your ability to accomplish what you want most, your success will inspire them to do the same. They will look to you as an example, encouraging them to pursue what sets their souls on fire. We see this happening between generations. When people nearing retirement clarify their goals and dreams, they become energized and excited, and their determination to reach specific goals inspires their children and grandchildren to find out what is most important to *them* in their lives. If you pursue what sets your soul on fire, you set a positive example for the next generation.

It can work the other way, too—young people who discover their big *why* in life can inspire the generations that came before them. Bryan considers his co-author and colleague at Sweet Financial Partners, Brittany, an amazing example of this positive influence. The people who get a chance to work with her through our coaching platform are attracted to her energy and drive. She keeps Bryan motivated as well, and she makes life fun. It's really a marvel to see a younger person exuding such positivity and focus. After spending thirty minutes with her, you're ready to climb Mount Everest!

Brittany, for example, appreciates Bryan's kind words. He asked her where her energy comes from, and she believes much of it comes from intentionality—making decisions that will expand her life beyond the status quo. To be clear, it's not necessarily about the pursuit of monetary goals or owning material things. Instead, Brittany wants to get as much out of this life as possible because we get only one go-round, so she wants to make it an exceptional one. She was also fortunate to have some key people in her life who truly believed in her from a very young age and who told her there was nothing she couldn't achieve if she put her mind to it.

That positive reinforcement inspired me. However, negative experiences as a young person can be inspiring, too. When you face dark and difficult times and are influenced by people with a negative mindset, we believe there are two choices you can make:

1. Fall into "victim mode," which will negatively influence your mindset.
2. Make the conscious decision to move forward in your life, with the drive to never feel that way again.

We prefer the second option! Negative experiences can inspire you to set goals and achieve them—to take control of your life—so you never have to be in that space again or feel that way again. The beauty of this is that you are in control. You get to decide how you react and respond to any and all circumstances that enter your life. Whether you are moving toward your best possible life or away from an undesirable situation, your conscious decision to pursue a specific dream will jump-start your journey.

Now, if the thought of inspiring other people—or an entire generation—sounds overwhelming, that's okay. If you can simply inspire yourself, you are making great progress.

When people say to him that they want to change the world, Joe Polish, founder of Genius Network®, responds, "Okay, show me how you've influenced one person first." It begins with one other person. And during difficult times like the COVID-19 pandemic, sometimes the only person you can influence is yourself, in your home. And that's still great! If you can change your awareness about the importance of setting clear goals and knowing what you want most in life, then you can begin to influence the people around you, one at a time.

NEGATIVITY EMERGED AS A PROTECTION MECHANISM IN OUR BRAINS

Science and human physiology help explain how much our mindset can affect our ability to succeed. Researchers John Gottman and Robert Levenson studied the effects of negativity on couples and discovered that it takes a minimum of five positive encounters to offset or counterbalance the impact of every negative encounter.[17]

The reticular activating system (RAS) of the human brain is sort of a neurological thermostat that measures our negative or positive emotions. When there is an overabundance of negative emotions, your RAS sees danger in all things, and it closes the parts of the brain where the more advanced cognitive processes, such as problem solving, exist. People who latch on to negative feelings seek to protect themselves from unsavory outcomes and uncertainty. Humans tend to prioritize negative or threatening things first and to see problems without considering the solutions. By thinking this way, they block the skills in the brain's RAS that help them solve problems and find

---

17   Bridget de Maine, "How Many Good Experiences Finally Outweigh a Bad One?" CollectiveHub, May 15, 2017, https://collectivehub.com/2017/05/how-many-good-experiences-finally-outweigh-a-bad-one.

long-term solutions. But when a healthy amount of positive emotions exists in the RAS, your brain receives the message that there's no danger, and the parts of the brain that close off when experiencing pessimistic emotions open up to receive an abundance of positivity.[18]

If you think back to our reference of the Baader-Meinhof phenomenon, your brain is wired to find evidence of whatever you're putting in front of it. If you're constantly saying, "Life is hard. Bad things keep happening to me. I can't catch a break. I'm never going to get ahead. I'm always going to be behind," then your brain will perceive those statements as facts. Your brain can't help but look for evidence to prove that you're right. Bombard yourself with positivity! If you change your thinking, you can change your results.

A MISTAKE IS NOT A FAILURE

Often, people are indecisive because they're afraid they will make the wrong decision. But making the wrong decision is better than making no decision at all, because you learn

---

18   Soulaima Gourani, "Is Your Mental Attitude Blocking Your Success?" *Forbes*, October 24, 2019, https://www.forbes.com/sites/soulaimagourani/2019/10/24/is-your-mental-attitude-blocking-your-success/#172ece42cd7c.

what *not* to do next time. Even if your decision turns out to be the wrong one, you can fix it. But you can't fix indecision.

Your desire to make the most of your future needs to outweigh any fear or what-if, such as, "What if this isn't the right decision?"

When things don't work out as well as they could have, we should not look at them as failures but rather as lessons learned. When we make mistakes, we now know something we didn't know before, so we can make better-educated decisions from that point forward.

In his book *The Power of Decision*, Raymond Charles Barker advises against letting a mistake define you. He stresses that we all have an innate, God-given intelligence that we need to tap into to make good decisions. He believes we each have the ability to shift the balance of decision-making power in our favor. He writes:

> Never judge yourself by what you have done. Judge yourself in terms of what you will do. You are not the past. You are the present becoming the future...The fact that you have made mistakes does not negate the fact that you are Intelligence in action. Every person living has made mistakes.[19]

---

19   Raymond Charles Barker, *The Power of Decision: A Step-by-Step Program...*

He also writes:

Every noteworthy achievement the world has ever seen was born with a single thought. Every great man or woman who ever lived has been one of decision.[20]

Instead of beating yourself up for making a less-than-ideal decision, acknowledge that now things will be better because you went through that experience and learned an important lesson. Weigh all the pros and cons of every option. Then make a decision, even if it's the wrong one. The very act of making a decision can have a powerful effect on your psyche.

FOCUS ON THE LONG TERM

When we look at the importance of making decisions and avoiding decisions that cannot be reversed, one of the barriers we often see when we begin working with clients in retirement planning is *short-term-itis*. In other words, people want instant results. They set goals and want results

---

...to Overcome Indecision and Live without Failure Forever (New York: TarcherPerigee, 2011), 6.

20   Barker, *The Power of Decision*, 6.

tomorrow. Bill Gates once said, "Most people overestimate what they can do in one year and underestimate what they can do in ten years."

When people don't get instant results, they often give up. They quit.

Don't quit! Focus on the long term, and follow the incremental goals in the plan that will get you where you want to go. Check in with your accountability partner often. Remind yourself of your personal values and what you want your legacy to be. Establish a regular routine that keeps your goals at the top of your mind. Whether you use a vision board or affirmations taped to your bathroom mirror, remind yourself often—we recommend daily—of the thing you want most in life. Focus on it, and it is more likely to manifest in your life.

Achieving your lifelong dream is an ongoing process. If you can understand that as part of the equation from the beginning, you will be more likely to reach your goal because you won't give up on yourself.

A SHINING EXAMPLE:
WALT DISNEY NEVER GAVE UP

There are many examples of well-known famous people who faced setbacks but never gave up—and then became wildly successful because they kept their eyes on their long-term goals.

At one point, Walt Disney was living on dog food (yes, you read that right), unable to pay his rent. Then his first character, Oswald the rabbit, was stolen. Next, MGM rejected his Mickey Mouse character on the basis that women are afraid of mice.[21] In 1919, Walt Disney was fired from the *Kansas City Star*. According to his editor, he "lacked imagination and had no good ideas." Disney then acquired Laugh-O-Gram, an animation studio he soon drove into bankruptcy. Finally, he decided to set his sights on a more profitable area: Hollywood.[22]

When he died in 1966, Walt Disney had a net worth equal to roughly $1 billion (after adjusting for inflation).[23] That's a lot of money, and it was a well-deserved outcome for a highly creative man who never gave up. He had a vision and he held tight to it!

---

21 Julie Ellis, "Never Giving Up: 9 Successful Entrepreneurs Who Failed at Least Once," Business.com, January 19, 2016, https://www.business.com/articles/never-giving-up-9-entrepreneurs-and-millionaires-who-failed-at-least-once.

22 Alana Horowitz, "15 People Who Were Fired before They Became Filthy Rich," Business Insider, April 25, 2011, https://www.businessinsider.com/15-people-who-were-fired-before-they-became-filthy-rich-2011-4.

23 "Walt Disney Net Worth," Celebrity Net Worth, accessed February 7, 2022, https://www.celebritynetworth.com/richest-businessmen/walt-disney-net-worth.

PLAN FOR THE EXPECTED—AND THE UNEXPECTED

Recently, we had a group of women do an exercise to help them discover their dreams and set priorities. One of the women shared a story about how she had it in her mind that she and her husband were going to travel in retirement. That had been a huge driver for her for her whole life. But now her parents were not doing well and they couldn't get around on their own. They needed help.

As we discussed in Chapter 1, it is important to clearly understand your personal values. The woman above is the perfect example of why this is important: when life interrupts your plans, you risk losing your way if those values are unclear or uncertain.

Let's say you decide taking care of family is your core value. That knowledge can guide decisions about balancing your dream of travel with the need to support aging parents. Keeping your family as the priority, we can build a financial plan that will take care of them—and potentially also allow you to travel in retirement.

As we have worked with clients through the COVID-19 pandemic, we have noticed that the people who have done their planning tend to have much less anxiety about COVID-19 than those who have not. The people who are nervous are the ones who haven't done the work. They have not determined what is most important to them in life. They have not discussed their dreams with an advisor. They haven't made the important decisions for their future and, in turn, don't know what their path is, even when the road is smooth. And during difficult times, they can't even find the road.

Sometimes interruptions in our plans provide opportunities we might have never considered if things had gone the way we wanted. For example, during the COVID-19 pandemic, many companies had to allow their employees to work from home. It's something many managers resisted because they feared losing control and the cohesion of their teams. But many of them are discovering that having people work from home has increased efficiency and employee well-being. What's more, they can increase their workforce without having to pay for more office space.

Recently, we were talking to some clients who own businesses about how giving people the opportunity to work from home has been great for business. The owners personally have improved their fitness and health because they're able to use their workout equipment at home more; they are making easily accessible exercise part of their daily routine. They also discovered that their employees are more highly engaged and less stressed.

It took a pandemic for many business owners and managers to realize the possibilities that, without a forcing action, may not have been realized. Much good can emerge from an unexpected situation. It all boils down to your mindset!

YOUR DECISION-MAKING TOOLBOX

1. If you've never done so before, write down your top three personal values. Then make every decision in a way that aligns with those values.

2. Do you find yourself thinking, *I always* ____, *I'm always* ____, or *I never* ____? If so, it's a good indication that you are reciting a narrative from long ago that no longer serves you well. Replace these statements with positive statements about yourself. Write them down and repeat them to yourself often.

3. Visit *www.mysweetfinancial.com* to access our Retirement Readiness Center and download

our proprietary Mindset Matters tool. This can help you identify the stressors in preparing for retirement and decide how those concerns can help you prepare for one of life's biggest transitions.

CHAPTER 3

STOP LETTING OTHERS "SHOULD" ON YOU

"Don't accept criticism from someone
you would never seek advice from."
—UNKNOWN

Before we get into the details of what it means to let someone "should" on you, it is important to remember that regardless of what anyone says, anything is possible. However, there are those among your acquaintances who may not be willing to affirm this and support you in your goals.

We have been talking about the importance of setting plans for your future, and we cannot stress enough how important it is to not let outside influences derail you from what you want most. We have seen it happen—clients let their friends, neighbors, or relatives tell them how they should set up their wealth plans or what they should or should not strive for in their future. This action is what we call letting others "should" on you. You cannot stop the naysayers from sharing their opinions with you, but you can control what you listen to and how you react. Although we believe most people have good intentions, sometimes their comments are not helpful.

If you have found yourself giving too much merit to the "should-ers" up to this point, we believe it is helpful to put blinders on and ignore those comments that would bring you down and keep you from pursuing what you want most. Keep your eyes on your own paper—focus on what you want. Then, as we have stressed, surround yourself with people who will support you and help you get there versus holding you back.

As the quote at the beginning of this chapter says, don't accept criticism from someone you would never seek advice from. If you know someone who has accomplished a lot and has done things you admire, that's the type of person you want to go to for advice. But people who time and time again seem to suck the life out of you, intentionally or not, are not people whose advice you should seek out.

Be keenly conscious of what's happening around you, what people are saying, and how it makes you feel. That is truly the first step to not getting "should" on—recognizing when a situation or environment is making you feel worse than when you arrived. In short, when you're not getting warm fuzzies, get up and move to a different room.

PEOPLE "SHOULD" ON US BECAUSE OF THEIR OWN SHORTCOMINGS

"People who lack the clarity, courage, or determination to follow their own dream will often find ways to discourage yours. Live your truth, and don't ever stop."
—Steve Maraboli

So why do some people feel the need to "should" on others, to offer their unsolicited opinions?

In many cases, those people are projecting their shortcomings onto others. Someone who hasn't accomplished what they want in life might subconsciously (or consciously for some) try to hinder you from achieving what you want most. They might be jealous of other people's big ideas and success. These people have a *scarcity* mentality—they believe there is only so much wealth and recognition to go around, so to get more for themselves, they have to keep others from getting ahead. People with an *abundance* mentality, on the other hand, believe there is enough wealth and recognition for everyone. These are the people who are happy to see others get ahead and will help them get ahead.

The people who tend to make negative comments about other people's dreams are often people who don't have clarity about their goals and whose fear holds them back.

People's attempts at sabotage can be damaging to us only if we listen to them.

CLARITY KEEPS US FROM LISTENING TO THE NAYSAYERS

In the planning we do for retirees, business owners, and women in transition, clarity is a huge factor in people's ability to transform a financial plan into reality. When you gain clarity about your purpose and passion, that enables you to filter out everything else, including other people's criticism. If you lack clarity about your purpose and path, you might be tempted to look for clarity from outside influences.

Let's say you're planning for retirement and you're not sure what that phase of life will look like for you. You will be more inclined to ask other people what they think you should do. That can be dangerous if you are seeking advice from the wrong people—the saboteurs. It can hinder your ability to really live your life to the fullest.

To be clear, we're not saying that a voice of reason here and there is a negative thing. We are recommending that you seek advice from those who have the best of intentions and really want you to fulfill your definition of success.

FOCUSING ON YOUR FUTURE IS LIBERATING

Some people spend their lives trying to please others, for whatever reason. But once you gain clarity about what you want in life, you can begin pleasing *yourself*. Retirement can be an incredibly liberating time. There is no boss to report to every day at work. You are no longer scrambling to meet or exceed clients' expectations. Your kids are grown and, hopefully, fending for themselves.

This is your time to shine! This is your time to be whole, and the only way you're going to feel whole is by focusing on yourself and what you want most.

One of the tools we use with our clients is the "over-din-ner conversation." We recommend that people discuss what they really want out of life with either their spouse or someone they trust has their best interest at heart. It helps couples get on the same page, both financially and otherwise.

The goal of this tool is to help individuals not only gain clarity on what they want most but to openly share their dreams with each other and to tell their loved ones how they can support. We completely understand that this can be an uncomfortable and sometimes difficult conversation to start because there is *so* much to think about when planning for your dream life. However, with careful thought, trust, and honesty, you can get the support you need and also be the support that your partner or trusted friend needs.

One of our clients recently became a widow. She had been married for decades, and her husband handled their money how he thought was best, without asking her what she wanted. She was comfortable with this arrangement because she didn't feel confident about her finances and trusted her husband. After he passed away, we sat down and worked with her to identify what she wanted and what her life could look like moving forward. Her finances were never something she thought she'd need to pay attention to. She did not realize that the plan that applied to both her and her husband might not be the same for just her. We helped her see that she can honor the life she had with her husband while designing a new path forward that will allow her to honor her own dreams.

When she met with us initially following her late husband's passing, she was feeling overwhelmed, faced with the fear of not knowing what retirement would now look like on her own. By simply refocusing on this new unanticipated future, she gained the confidence to know that even though life is now different, she is going to be okay. And although her dreams may feel distant at the outset, she now knows that when the time is right, she will reach them again.

It is natural for our goals and dreams to shift as we navigate transitions in life. We also see this with divorced couples. One spouse who has let the other one make all the decisions about the future suddenly gets a chance to focus on their desires. It is incredibly rewarding to watch people discover what they love and enjoy in life, after years of deferring to others. Finally, they can focus on what they want as individuals versus what they wanted as a couple.

This is why it is so incredibly important for both spouses to meet with their advisor. You never know when a major transition can happen. Even though you may not have a big drive to know the ins and outs of your financial plan, you should at least have your goals and dreams on the table to make sure both you and your partner get the most out of life.

Loss happens and loved ones can pass suddenly. If this happens to you, know that you're always going to miss the person who was important to you, but please know that there is abundance ahead of you as well. Life might not look like what you had envisioned, but there is still so much that's possible. You can still realize your full potential even when life throws an ugly curveball at you.

We have helped many people navigate difficult transitions. They have told us it gives them strength and solace to know we are in their corner, supporting them and helping them discover what the next normal looks like.

THE STORY YOU BELIEVE IS THE STORY THAT WILL PLAY OUT IN YOUR LIFE

What you look for in life is what you get. If you are looking for reasons why you *can't* do something, they will appear. If you are looking for reasons why you *can* do something, they will appear. Whatever story you fixate on could end up being the story that's going to play out.

Years ago, after a company meeting, Bryan was having a cigar and a cocktail with the president of Raymond James Financial Services. He said, "Bryan, you really have the ability to be one of the best advisors in our system."

At the time, Bryan was doing okay, but he wasn't really in the "best" category. The year after that discussion, he was ranked among the top advisors in the company he was with at the time,[24] and he stayed there the entire time he was with that company—largely because the president of the company told Bryan he believed in him. That simple vote of confidence was what helped him to believe in himself more than he ever had. To this day, Bryan still thinks about those encouraging words. They are a big contributing factor in why he constantly seeks to improve and excel in serving him and Brittany's clients.

Sometimes we need to give ourselves permission to go after what we've always wanted—and many times, that doesn't happen until someone we admire expresses belief in our potential.

NEGATIVITY BIAS CAUSES US TO FOCUS ON NEGATIVE MESSAGES

So why do we often believe the negative story instead of the positive version?

In Chapter 2, we described how the reticular activating system (RAS) in the human brain causes people to latch on to negative feelings to protect themselves from

---

24 Raymond James Chairman's Council from 2004–2021. Membership is based on prior fiscal year production. Requalification is required annually. This recognition is not indicative of the advisor's future performance, is not an endorsement, and may not be representative of individual client experiences.

unsavory outcomes and uncertainty. This scientific phenomenon explains the concept of "negativity bias," or a tendency to focus on negative messaging more than positive messaging.

Research confirms this. The National Science Foundation has reported that 80 percent of our thoughts in any given day are negative. And 95 percent of our thoughts are exactly the same thoughts from yesterday.[25] Nobel Prize-winning researchers Daniel Kahneman and Amos Tversky found that when making decisions, people consistently place greater weight on negative aspects of an event than they do on positive ones.[26]

Laura Mixon Camacho, PhD, a communication coach at Mixonian Institute, says, "The human brain remembers negative messages, results, and possibilities with greater magnitude than positive ones." The negativity bias originally served a strong evolutionary purpose. In prehistoric times, remaining alert for potential danger was the key to surviving. But, Camacho says, "modern times favor

---

25 Neringa Antanaityte, "Mind Matters: How to Effortlessly Have More Positive Thoughts," TLEX Institute, accessed February 7, 2022, https://tlexinstitute.com/how-to-effortlessly-have-more-positive-thoughts.

26 Daniel Kahneman and Amos Tversky, "Choices, Values, and Frames," *American Psychologist* 39, no. 4 (1984): 341–350, https://doi.org/10.1037/0003-066X.39.4.341.

humans who not only imagine a better future but who put in the work to make it become reality. Fixating on negative possibilities creates harmful stress that actually shortens lifespans."[27]

So although negativity bias may have served us well in the past, it doesn't serve us well now. We must work on deprogramming our brains from this natural bias.

NOT EVERYONE WILL LOVE US, AND THAT'S OKAY

Think of a time in your life when you achieved something that got you 99.9 percent praise, but a single naysayer completely deflated your confidence.

Brittany has had the great privilege to speak on stages across the United States, and after many of her presentations, the audience was able to rate or grade the presentation and give comments about it. She vividly remembers getting the results after one particular talk during which she not only gave her all but also shared a personal story to help drive the point home. She received rave reviews from every person in attendance—except for one. And

---

27   Laura Camacho, "Four Ways Negativity Bias Slows You Down (and How to Stop It)," *Forbes*, February 26, 2019, https://www.forbes.com/sites/forbescoachescouncil/2019/02/26/four-ways-negativity-bias-slows-you-down-and-how-to-stop-it/#50de40d4c5f9.

you know which comment she remembers verbatim? The comment from the one person who said her talk felt like a "canned speech." That one negative comment kept Brittany from focusing on the high number of positive comments she received.

She was really down on herself, so she sought out one of her speaking coaches. He told her, "Brittany, as lovable as you are, not everyone is going to like you." That was a real eye-opener for her. No matter how much effort you put in, there will always be someone who will have something to say that stings a little bit.

The truth is, we're never going to please all the people all the time. We would be doing ourselves a huge favor if we could change that narrative and focus on all the rave reviews we've received in our lifetime.

Now, we don't normally quote burlesque performers, but we're making an exception here. We love this quote by well-known burlesque performer Dita Von Teese: "You could be the ripest, juiciest peach in the whole world, and there's still going to be somebody who hates peaches."

We don't need everyone to love us, and we don't need to know why some might not. It's just a fact of life. At the beginning of this book, we clearly stated that we know it will not be for everyone. But we have enough faith to know that the ones whom it *is* written for will get a lot out of it.

The same understanding can be applied to anything you are working toward.

Focus on the people who appreciate you, know your true intentions, and support your journey. Avoid focusing on those people who bring you down.

We've all heard the saying, "You can't teach an old dog new tricks." We don't believe that's true. You have the opportunity to rewrite your story at any given point in time. Many people discovered their true calling and achieved phenomenal success later in life. If they had quit, they never would have accomplished big things. If you have always believed the naysayers and focused on the negative messages, we encourage you to change that approach. Focus on the positive, and let us help you.

Know what you want, make a plan for achieving it, and be intentional with your actions. Make the conscious choice to forge your path ahead.

CHALLENGE ACCEPTED!

If a naysayer inflicts their negativity on you, you can respond by saying, "I appreciate what you're saying, but I am clear about my goals, and I know that if I put my mind to it, I can get there." You have only one life—don't spend it reacting to someone else's judgment. Strive for what you want and tune out everything else. It is important to remember that not everything needs a reaction. It's up to you to preserve your energy *pursuing* your biggest dreams, not *defending* them.

When the naysayer is a close family member or friend, the dynamics of your relationship can be sensitive. In most cases, you can't remove those people from your life, and you don't have to. It isn't even necessary to tell them they're bad people; just *stop listening* to them.

There have been times when Brittany's close family members told her, "You'll never do that" or "Let's stop kidding ourselves." She didn't let their words get her down, though. When people make comments like these, Brittany is wired to say, "Challenge accepted." That might be her stubbornness shining through, but she really encourages you to embrace this mindset. If you want something badly enough, nothing in this world should slow you down from your pursuit!

When someone throws a "you should" or "you shouldn't" your way, just tell yourself—and them—"Challenge accepted!"

It is important to know that the only time you fail is when you quit. As long as you keep that in mind, when you want something bad enough, you're never going to quit. And that's all that matters.

In her bestselling 1992 self-help book, *A Return to Love*, spiritual leader Marianne Williamson wrote a much-quoted passage that is incredibly empowering:

> Our deepest fear is not that we're inadequate. Our deepest fear is that we are powerful beyond measure. It is our light, not our darkness, that most frightens us. We ask ourselves, Who am I to be brilliant, gorgeous, talented, fabulous? Actually, who are you not to be? Your playing small does not serve the world. There is nothing enlightened about shrinking so that other people won't feel insecure around you. We are all meant to shine, as children do...And as we let our own light shine, we unconsciously give other people permission to do the same. As we are liberated from our own fear, our presence automatically liberates others.[28]

If you allow yourself to be all those wonderful things, what could your life look like? Imagine the possibilities!

Is the glass half full, or is it half empty? All that matters is that the glass can be filled again. You might be at a point in your life where there's a ton of opportunity ahead of

---

28 Marianne Williamson, *A Return to Love: Reflections on the Principles of a Course in Miracles* (New York: HarperCollins, 1992).

you. Or you may be experiencing struggle at this point in your life. But all that matters is that you keep your eye on the prize and continue to fill that cup. Pour good things into your days and into your thoughts. Pay attention to those people, things, and messages that will encourage you to move forward in a way that honors your success and dreams. Filter out everything else that's negative. If you fill your life with positivity, your cup will fill up again and you will feel whole.

NEXT STEPS

By the way, as we focus on deflecting the "shoulds" that other people throw our way, we need to make sure we don't "should" on others. In the spirit of mutual respect, let's make sure we don't let our fears spill over into the advice we give to others or into the way we show up for others. Be mindful of this tendency.

YOUR TOOLBOX FOR FIGHTING
OFF THE "SHOULDS"

1. Ask yourself, "What are the things I'm doing, or not doing, in my life only because it's what others think I should or should not be doing?" Now use the space below to write down some of the items that came to mind.

_____

_____

_____

_____

_____

2. Go to *www.mysweetfinancial.com* to access our proprietary tool, The Lies We Tell Ourselves, located in Retirement Readiness. This will help you identify what is holding you back from the life you desire and the steps you need to ignore

the naysayers while building positive support around you.

3. When you find yourself fixating on negative thoughts or negative comments from others, one quick way to come out of that bunker is to focus on gratitude. Look up *Imagine. Act. Inspire. A Daily Journal* on Amazon.com to order your copy of our gratitude journal.

4. Look through the quotes we have included in this chapter and in the rest of the book. Does one of them resonate deeply with you? If so, print it out or write it down, and place it somewhere you will see it every day. The more you read, listen to, and focus on positive messages, the more you'll start believing them, and the more you'll start acting with those messages in mind.

CHAPTER 4

YOU ARE THE AVERAGE OF THE FIVE PEOPLE YOU SURROUND YOURSELF WITH

"You are the average of the five people
you spend the most time with."

—JIM ROHN

As the quote above states, we tend to adopt the same mindsets and behaviors of the five people we're around the most. For that reason, we need to spend time with people who support and encourage us—people who don't "should" on us, as we discussed in Chapter 3. People can either lift you up or bring you down.

If you notice that you're having negative thoughts or a bad attitude, and if you are living a fear-based life versus an abundant life, look who you are allowing into your circle of influence. It's possible that the people around you are contributing to your negative outlook and squelching your joy about the future. They are not necessarily bad people, but spending time with them might not be good for your psyche and your personal growth. Notice how the people around you respond when you share a big goal or dream with them. Do they respond by saying things like, "You can't do that" or "That seems ridiculous"? Even if they are not sabotaging your efforts directly, you could probably benefit from spending less time with those who are not supporting you.

Now, in contrast, notice the people in your business and personal life who are excited for you when you share a goal with them and who have their own ambitious goals for the future. Between the two groups, which people are striving to be better and are pushing you to be the best version of yourself? Which group tends to take on new challenges, try new things, stretch their capabilities, and encourage you to do the same?

When we spend a great deal of time with people, we tend to emulate them. If they're not good influences on us, we can fall into patterns that are not aligned with our goals.

Let's say you're on a personal health journey. You really want to focus on your diet and exercise. You go out to dinner with friends, and they're all ordering the fried appetizers, pizzas, and huge desserts. It can be easy to get caught up in doing what everyone else is doing, but succumbing to the peer pressure will get you off track from your personal health journey.

Maybe you're with a few people who start talking about the news, politics, and all the horrible things going on in the world. Maybe they are gossiping about other people. If that's something you don't want to be a part of, you will need to separate yourself from that conversation—and maybe from those people.

Surround yourself with people who remind you of your future self, not your past or present self. Spend your time around people who talk about ideas and the future, people who encourage and support you as you work to achieve your vision for the future. If the people around you are not supportive of that, it might be time for you to take a step back and reassess how you're allocating your time. Remember what Eleanor Roosevelt said: "Great minds discuss ideas; average minds discuss events; small minds discuss people."

WHAT IF YOU'VE NEVER EXPERIENCED SUPPORT FROM OTHERS?

Not everybody was raised with positive, uplifting people around them. Negative circumstances trap many people in a negative, demoralizing environment. A child who grows up around toxic people is likely to follow that pattern and become a toxic adult.

If that has been your experience, think back to when you were a child. What type of person would you have loved to be around? Do you currently know or know of anyone who has the type of positive influence you could have benefited from as a child? Why not be that person yourself? Ayesha Siddiqi said, "Be the person you needed when you were younger."

If you have never experienced support, you can start by being your biggest fan.

As we design the types of retirement people can't wait to wake up to, they often tell us that spending time with their families and providing for future generations is important to them. If your family experience growing up was far from positive, you can change your story and your family's story. Let the legacy of negativity stop with you, and change the narrative of your future.

To attract positive people into your life, start by becoming the uplifting, positive, supportive person you would like to have near you. If you need a cheerleader, become that for yourself or for someone else.

You are much better off being alone than being around toxic or negative people. Don't settle for less-than-supportive people in your life just because you want company. Life will treat you much better if you completely get away from those folks as much as you can. Seek out people who are like the person you want to be in the future.

ADOPT SMALL HABITS FIRST

Expecting big changes in our lives overnight, such as changing our core group of friends and influencers, is unrealistic. You don't have to replace several close friends overnight. We recommend starting out by cultivating *one* positive relationship in your life. Set that intention in your mind. (As we mentioned earlier, your brain will seek out whatever intention you set.)

In his 2019 book, *Tiny Habits*, B. J. Fogg explains that when we put pressure on ourselves to accomplish too much, we become overwhelmed and procrastinate. A much more effective strategy, he says, is to build tiny habits that reinforce behavior change.

Fogg writes:

We live in an aspiration-driven culture that is rooted in instant gratification. We find it difficult to enact or even accept incremental progress. Which is exactly what you need to cultivate meaningful long-term change. People get frustrated and demoralized when things don't happen quickly. It's natural. It's normal. But it's another way we're set up to fail.

He adds, "Over the last twenty years, I've found that the only consistent, sustainable way to grow big is to start small."[29]

You can make small changes each morning that will start your day off with a positive vibe. Instead of tackling your email in-box right away or doom-scrolling the news, which can be stressful, read a positive quote. Think about or write down three people and things you are grateful for. Tell yourself an affirmation—for example, "It's going to be a great day." Even small actions like these can set the stage for the rest of your day.

Once you've adopted a few small habits, consider expanding your positive morning routine to half an hour. During that time, read books and blog posts, listen to

---

29   B. J. Fogg, *Tiny Habits: The Small Changes That Change Everything* (Boston: Houghton Mifflin Harcourt, 2019), 8.

podcasts, and watch videos (such as TED Talks) that are informative and positive. Then, when you engage in conversations with people, your mind will be full of interesting ideas, and you will exude optimism. As Gandhi said, "As a man changes his own nature, so does the attitude of the world change towards him."

If you fill your mind with positive, uplifting thoughts and information, you will be likely to attract positive people into your life.

REACH OUT TO PEOPLE
YOU WANT TO KNOW

Many people are not intentional about the people they spend time with. People come into their lives as childhood friends, neighbors, coworkers, or in-laws, and they just accept that those are the people in their circles of influence. But you can be more intentional about choosing the people you surround yourself with.

Identify people you admire and respect—people you want to emulate—and reach out to them. Depending on the situation, you might reach out in person or on an online forum like LinkedIn. Simply tell them that you admire them, and explain what you're trying to accomplish. Most people will be flattered and will agree to give you some helpful ideas or insights, maybe in one or more brief phone conversations.

Don't be afraid to reach out. Some people might say they don't have time to help you, but if you ask five people to spend a few minutes with you on the phone, three will probably say yes.

If someone does say yes and you plan a phone call, have several specific questions ready. Busy people will probably find it frustrating if the conversation gets off to a slow start. At some point, be sure to thank them for their time and insights.

Recently, Brittany was on a call with a woman from another financial advisory office. She was looking for some insight into how to juggle being a parent and having a career. She felt overwhelmed with the expectation to fulfill every role well. During their hour on the phone, Brittany answered her questions and encouraged her. The next day, the woman sent her a beautiful bouquet of flowers with a card that was just so touching. Brittany was blown away that spending one hour of her time could make such a difference in her life. It reminded her that people often need a boost, and you might be the only person accessible to them who can provide it.

BALANCE YOUR NEEDS WITH OTHERS' NEEDS

We have run across individuals who don't even realize the people around them are stifling their potential joy and prosperity. For example, when you look at planning for your retirement, it is incredibly important to identify what means you will need to support the life that will be most fulfilling to you. But issues can arise when the future retiree is more concerned with supporting a family member—whether an adult child or more distant relative—at the sacrifice of their own success or fulfillment.

This is why it's essential for us to truly understand what our clients want most in this life, as decisions that may feel good in the moment can have a long-term negative effect on their financial picture. It's hard to recover from that type of damage once it's done. This is just one more benefit to having a trusted, competent, compassionate advisor to help you design your retirement and stay on track. Sometimes we can see dynamics that our clients cannot see because they are too close to the situation. We attempt to give you an unbiased assessment of what is likely to happen if you make a certain financial decision, such as cashing out your 401(k) account to help an adult child who has always relied on the help of their parents and continually asks for help. We will encourage you to keep your dreams at the top of your priority list and discourage you from allowing someone to influence your thoughts, opinions, and actions regarding your finances.

As we discussed earlier, it all goes back to defining your values. This is why it is critical to get crystal clear about what you want out of life. Once you do that, it's easy to determine if each action you consider is in line with the values you said are important to you. If you keep your eyes on your values, it will be easy to see when someone else's pleas for help are likely to disrupt your path forward. You have only one life to live. Loving and respecting your family does not include letting them influence you in a negative way and derailing all that you've worked so hard to achieve.

WE ARE COMMITTED TO HELPING SINGLE MOMS

Many times, single moms are particularly vulnerable to letting their children talk them into financial moves that are not ideal for the moms' future plans. That is why we offer complimentary financial plans for single moms through our Women Forward platform. We are committed to empowering and educating women about their finances and their personal well-being.

Both of us understand firsthand what it means to be raised by a single mom. Many single moms have little support, and they devote all their time, money, and energy to making sure they raise their children well. We have found that as a result, many single moms have never thought about what *they* want for the future. Their focus is always on their children. We want women to understand that it's okay, and even necessary, to look out for their own well-being. And it's okay to push back if someone close to you—even one of your children—is having a toxic influence on you and your financial future.

For many parents, their number one value is family. Their kids are their most important priority. That makes perfect sense, but we want to make sure that people are not providing for their adult children to the exclusion of their own needs. We have seen people delay retirement to help their adult kids buy homes or continue their college education. If the parents have limited resources, this might not be a wise move. Their children might have twenty-five to forty years to continue earning money, whereas the parents are on the cusp of retirement and need that money to live on soon.

There are many different scenarios we can help you explore so that you are contributing to your children while still taking care of yourself. This is an important topic to discuss with your advisor. We will be your accountability partner and help keep you on track to reach your goals.

It doesn't have to be either-or. You can take care of your loved ones and yourself with careful planning. We will help you make informed decisions that balance your personal needs with your desire to help others. We won't tell you that you can't do something, but we will remind you of your values and help you stay on track with the financial plan we have developed together.

HOW TO STEP AWAY FROM NEGATIVE PEOPLE

If you have realized that one or more of the five people closest to you have been influencing you negatively or not supporting your goals and dreams, it might be time to distance yourself from them.

You could be "busy" every time the person wants to get together. Or you could be more honest and have a difficult conversation with that person. If you decide to take this route, be prepared for them to become defensive, especially if you say you want to cut ties completely. If it's a family member, you probably won't want to cut ties completely; you might just want that person to understand how their comments are affecting you.

If you have this conversation, we recommend gathering your thoughts before talking to the person. Then, when you see them, say there's something you'd like to discuss.

Begin by framing the situation in a way that does not assign blame to the other person. You could say something like, "When you [*describe what the person says or does*], it makes me feel [*describe how it makes you feel*]." After you have finished describing how you feel, thank the person for listening and give them a chance to respond.

You cannot control how somebody receives what you say, but you can control your delivery and the way you handle their response. Whatever method you use to distance yourself from toxic people, give yourself a pat on the back for taking a huge step toward achieving your best future!

At Sweet Financial, our goal is to be among the five people you should find who help you get to where you want to go. We will encourage you every step of the way.

YOUR TOOLBOX FOR SURROUNDING YOURSELF WITH POSITIVE PEOPLE WHO WILL ENCOURAGE YOU

1. Below, list the five people you spend the most time with. Then indicate, by choosing a number

between 1 and 10, how positive or negative their influence is, with 1 being the most negative and 10 being the most positive.

a. Person 1: _____

b. Person 2: _____

c. Person 3: _____

d. Person 4: _____

e. Person 5: _____

2. Now list five people you admire deeply who either have had a positive impact in your life personally or have contributed to the world in a positive way. Write down the qualities you admire about them.

_____

_____

_____

_____

_____

3. Which of these five people would you reach out to for ideas and insight as you strive to reach personal or business-related goals?

CHAPTER 5

GET OUT OF YOUR OWN WAY

"You are far too smart to be the only
thing standing in your way."
—JENNIFER J. FREEMAN

We've talked about how others can impact your ability to achieve your dreams, but what about that person looking back at you in the mirror? To what extent do you support and encourage yourself?

Often, people are their own worst enemies: the biggest limitation we typically have is the six inches between our ears—our minds. Fear, self-doubt, and uncertainty can prevent us from achieving our potential and our dreams. Negative self-talk is detrimental, too. Would you allow anyone to talk to you the way you talk to yourself? Probably not!

We all need to discover where and how we are limiting ourselves. We need to get out of our own way and allow ourselves to succeed.

THE POWER OF SELF-BELIEF

Darren Hardy tells a story in one of his Darren Daily videos about a high school student who was doing terribly in school. It was causing frustration for his parents, so he promised his mom he would at least take his SATs to see if he could get into college. The scores came back, and he got a 1480, which is uncommonly high—a perfect score is 1600. All of a sudden, the kid was excelling in school. His teachers were saying, "Oh my gosh, we had this kid completely wrong."

He started hanging out around different people; the friends he had before weren't exactly 1480-type friends. He got into college, and everything was going well for him. Then one day, he found out that the people who had scored his SAT messed up on his results—he had actually scored a 740, not a 1480. But because he *saw* himself as someone who scored 1480, it made a huge difference in his mindset and behavior. After college, this young man became a highly successful magazine executive and did amazingly well.[30]

Again, whatever you believe about yourself will manifest. Decide what you want out of life, believe you can achieve it, and surround yourself with people who challenge you to achieve it.

BE INTENTIONAL ABOUT YOUR SUCCESS

In Chapter 4, we mentioned the importance of starting each day on a positive note and adopting a routine of reading, watching, or listening to positive material. You can expand on that time by setting intentions that will move you closer to what you want most.

Dr. Benjamin P. Hardy recommends taking the following steps to get yourself into a positive mindset:

1. Meditate.
2. Set your intentions.
3. Be present.

---

30 Darren Daily videos expire after three days and cannot be viewed again afterward. https://go.darrenhardy.com/darrendaily.

4. Do everything with purpose.

5. Find love within yourself and others.

6. Move your body.

7. Invest in your passion.

In his book *The Miracle Morning*, Hal Elrod says you should always start your morning by taking care of yourself and getting into the right mental state before tackling your day. He calls his suggested routine "Life SAVERS."[31] Here are the steps that make up the acronym SAVERS:

- Silence
- Affirmations
- Visualization
- Exercise
- Reading
- Scribing

All these activities contribute to your personal well-being. The time you take each morning is for you alone—time to focus on what you really want out of life and how you will achieve it. It doesn't necessarily matter how you

31   Hal Elrod, *The Miracle Morning: The Not-So-Obvious Secret Guaranteed to Transform Your Life (before 8AM)* (N.p.: Miracle Morning Publishing, 2012).

go about this as long as you commit to a routine and follow it every single day. Use the ideas above as guidelines and find something you can stick to.

EXERCISE IMPROVES OUR OUTLOOK AND HEALTH

All the components of a morning routine are important, but we especially want to discuss how critical exercise is in improving your physical, mental, and emotional health.

Many studies show, for example, that exercise diminishes the effects of depression. According to Dr. Michael Craig Miller, assistant professor of psychiatry at Harvard Medical School, exercising starts a biological cascade of events that results in many health benefits, such as protecting against heart disease and diabetes, improving sleep, and lowering blood pressure. For most of us, the real value is in low-intensity exercise sustained over time. That kind of activity spurs the release of proteins called neurotrophic or growth factors, which cause nerve cells to grow and make new connections. The improvement in brain function makes you feel better. Dr. Miller writes:

In people who are depressed, neuroscientists have noticed that the hippocampus in the brain—the region that helps regulate mood—is smaller. Exercise supports nerve cell growth in the hippocampus, improving nerve cell connections, which helps relieve depression.[32]

Like the other components of a morning routine, exercising can become a habit over time. It might be difficult to stick to your routine at first. But if you commit to the routine for, say, a month, then at the end of that month, it's likely that your routine has become a natural part of your morning that you look forward to. Consistency is the key. Do these activities every day, and they will become positive habits that benefit you in many ways. Start small and then build from there. Remember Lao Tzu's saying, "A journey of a thousand miles begins with a single step."

FOCUS ON WHAT MATTERS MOST

During your morning routine, focus on your purpose and plan your day in a way that intentionally moves you toward that purpose. Whatever life stage you are in, we think you will benefit from adopting a morning routine.

---

32 "Exercise Is an All-Natural Treatment to Fight Depression," *Harvard Health Letter*, updated March 25, 2019, https://www.health.harvard.edu/mind-and-mood/exercise-is-an-all-natural-treatment-to-fight-depression.

Now, of course things happen that are beyond our control, and these circumstances can delay our progress. We certainly saw that happen in 2020 like no other time in recent history. But if you know what you want, you will find a way to move past the obstacles that life throws at you. If you don't know what you want and what your purpose is, then external forces can cause you to lose your way completely.

It's easy to get distracted when life is coming at you fast. We pay attention to what other people are doing and saying, and we let everyday noise and hullabaloo take our focus off our goals. Try to tune out those distractions so you can focus on what you want most and what actions you need to take to move toward those dreams.

Have you ever heard of the Pareto principle, also known as the 80/20 rule? It's named after economist Vilfredo Pareto, who was born in 1848. The rule states that 80 percent of results come from just 20 percent of action. Through the past century and a half, many people have written about this phenomenon. For example, in 1999, Richard Koch published *The 80/20 Principle*. He explains how we can achieve much more with much less effort, time, and resources simply by identifying and focusing our efforts on the 20 percent that really counts.

Tune out the 80 percent that doesn't matter and focus on the 20 percent that does. Once you set your goal and figure out the steps you need to reach that goal, don't let anything distract you from completing those steps.

WRITE DOWN WHO AND
WHAT YOU'RE GRATEFUL FOR

The morning routine we recommend in Chapter 4 is an ideal time to focus on your dreams. Visualize them, plan them, and write down actions you will take that day to get you there. You might be amazed at how much progress you make toward what you want most in life through the simple act of writing it down and placing intentional focus on those desires.

We know from personal experience that if you focus first thing in the morning on how to accomplish your goals, this will set the path for your day, which, in turn, sets the path for your week, your month, your year, and so forth.

In 2017, we published a daily journal titled *Imagine. Act. Inspire.* We designed it specifically for getting focused on what's most important to you. Each day starts you off with a positive quote to help you practice positive thinking. There is also space to write down two gratitudes and three to-do items for the day. Taken together, this combination of positivity, gratitude, and mindful preparation will help you start the day on the right foot.

Gratitude is an important component of having a positive outlook. No matter what happens to us and no matter how defeated we feel, we can always find people and things to be grateful for.

Author Benjamin Hardy, PhD, says gratitude journaling is a scientifically proven way to overcome some psychological challenges. He lists many benefits of gratitude, including the following:[33]

- Gratitude makes you happier.
- Gratitude strengthens your emotions.
- Gratitude makes you more optimistic.
- Gratitude helps you bounce back from challenges.
- Gratitude helps you relax.
- Gratitude makes you friendlier.
- Gratitude helps your marriage.

Writing down your top three to-dos is a great way to keep you focused on your goals. One thing we often do to get in our own way is to bite off more than we can chew. Brittany has been guilty of creating a to-do list that has

---

33   Benjamin Hardy, "Unsuccessful People Focus on 'the Gap.' Here's What Successful People Focus On," LinkedIn, August 14, 2020, https://www. linkedin.com/pulse/unsuccessful-people-focus-gap-heres-what-successful-hardy-phd/?trackingId=K9W5toy3REmGTGL%2BotoNkg%3D%3D.

seventy-five items on it because she's an eternal optimist. She thinks she can do it all, all the time. What would happen is that she'd get to the end of the day, and if she had completed only a couple of those items, she tended to feel like she didn't accomplish much.

If you're guilty of this "overachiever" type of thought process, the good news is, there is a better way to do it. Focus on just three things. Ask yourself, "What's going to move the needle? What actions are going to get me to where I want to be faster, more efficiently, or more effectively?" Then, when you accomplish those three things, you will feel better about your progress.

MEASURE PROGRESS AGAINST YOUR PREVIOUS PLACE IN LIFE

Measuring our progress is important. Many times, we either fail to measure our progress at all, or we measure our progress in unrealistic ways.

In his book *The Gap and the Gain*, Dan Sullivan explains that your ideals and goals are very different. *Ideals* are general and immeasurable and constantly change. Your ideals should not be your benchmark for achievement; instead, they should be the source from which you create your specific, challenging, time-bound, and measurable *goals.* He says that if you measure your current self against your ideal, you'll never be happy because there will always be a gap.

Instead, Sullivan recommends measuring your current self against your previous self—where you were when you set your goals (and even before). He stresses that if you're not making progress, you can't feel confident, because confidence is a by-product of prior success. And if you don't regularly take the time to review your progress, you'll never appreciate the small details, which will rob you of the experience and all the benefits of gratitude.[34]

JUST BE PRESENT

Many times, we get in our own way by constantly thinking, maybe even worrying, about all the stuff we need to get done. We don't allow ourselves to just be present and enjoy the moment.

We have seen people who are newly retired have a difficult time winding down from their frenetic careers. They have lived their entire lives reacting to the hustle and bustle of work and raising families. They have never learned to just be present and think about what they want most.

---

34   Hardy, "Unsuccessful People Focus on 'the Gap.'"

It's great to be a high achiever, but don't let the act of chasing achievements rob you of the joy of profoundly simple moments enjoying your life.

As Bill Gates said, people tend to overestimate what they can accomplish in the short term and underestimate what they can do in the longer term. They get frustrated in the short run if things don't turn out exactly the way they anticipate, whereas the outcome might have been better if they had allowed more time for the ideal outcome to materialize. Sometimes we need to just take a deep breath and let things fall into place without trying to control them.

SAY NO SOMETIMES

We absolutely believe in giving to others, but sometimes it's possible to give so much that you are causing yourself harm.

Burnout is a very real phenomenon, and it often manifests when we're making too many "withdrawals" from our personal bank of energy and not making enough "deposits." Although it's admirable to give to others, be careful you don't give so much that you deplete the stores of energy you need to move toward your goals.

In many cases, the solution to burnout is to simply say no. Be selective about the committees or boards you serve on, the favors you do for friends and neighbors, and the help you give your loved ones. Say no to people, obligations, requests, and opportunities that you're either not interested in or will not help you get to where you want to go. Billionaire and Berkshire Hathaway CEO Warren Buffett once said, "The difference between successful people and really successful people is that really successful people say no to almost everything."

When we say yes to everything, we need to ask ourselves, "Who am I really trying to please?" If you are volunteering for everything because you think you are not enough as you are, that is an example of getting in your own way. Know that you are enough just as you are—God doesn't make junk! Again, knowing what you want most out of life will make it easy for you to discern which opportunities to say yes to and which ones to turn down.

Saying no doesn't make you selfish; it just means you're focused. To live a fulfilled life requires making wise choices about how you spend your time, energy, and money.

DON'T QUIT BECAUSE YOU'RE DISCOURAGED

In his classic book *Think and Grow Rich*, Napoleon Hill tells the story of a man who dug for gold in a mine out west. After a few weeks, he saw some shining ore but realized he needed equipment to bring it to the surface. He concealed the mine, returned to Maryland, and his family put together money for some equipment, which they shipped to him out west when he returned. His initial efforts looked promising, but then the ore seemed to vanish. Discouraged, he gave up and sold his equipment to a junk dealer for a few hundred dollars. It turned out that the original miner was only *three feet* from a huge deposit of ore. The junk dealer made millions from the ore he mined after the first man gave up.[35]

Of course, it is discouraging when things don't go the way that we want or expect. But if you quit when you get discouraged, you'll never reach your goal, which might be closer than you think. As John Greenleaf Whittier's famous poem "Don't Quit" says, "When care is pressing you down a bit, rest if you must, but don't you quit."

When something bad happens, you have three choices. You can either let it define you, you can let it destroy you, or you can let it strengthen you. Quitting is what we call a *possibility killer*. Be aware of how you handle disappointment. Try to boost your resilience through positive self-talk, affirmations, and the other positive actions we've recommended for your morning routine and beyond.

---

35 Napoleon Hill, *Think and Grow Rich* (New York: TarcherPerigee, 2005), 5–6.

DON'T MAKE EXCUSES

One thing people do to get in their own way is to make excuses for why they haven't attempted or accomplished something. Jim Rohn, American author, entrepreneur, and motivational speaker, says, "If you really want to do something, you'll find a way. If you don't, you'll find an excuse." You must commit to what you want and go after it.

Now, sometimes our excuses are valid; we consider them reasons, not excuses. In most cases, however, excuses are self-appointed, merely a way to avoid moving toward goals. As Grant Cardone, author of *The 10X Rule*, says, "Your excuses might be legit, but they won't improve your life."

It is incredibly important to understand that to live an abundant life filled with opportunities and experiences, both big and small, we must not allow our excuses to get in the way.

STRIVE FOR EXCELLENCE, NOT PERFECTION

Are you a perfectionist? Don't be! Strive for excellence instead, because perfection isn't possible unless you're God. When you are working on a project, be happy with 80 percent of the details being just as you want them; trying to get 100 percent of them perfect is an exercise in futility that will only frustrate you.

Many times, people become seized by "analysis paralysis." They become overwhelmed with the options, data, or details in front of them, and then they don't do anything because they're afraid to make the wrong choice. Trust yourself. Trust that you will make the best decision you can at that moment. Know that even if you make the wrong decision, then, as we've said earlier in the book, you have learned something valuable, nonetheless. Take action so you can move forward and make progress. Don't worry if your outcome isn't perfect; you can course correct as you go. But if you don't take any steps, there will be no course to correct.

TALK TO YOURSELF WITH RESPECT

If somebody walked into your house and started insulting you, you would say, "Get the heck out of my house! Who are you to say that to me?"

But we say terrible things to ourselves all the time. We chastise ourselves for making what we consider a mistake or for getting off track from our goals. Or we tell ourselves, "You're not smart enough to achieve that goal" or "That is an unrealistic dream."

We wouldn't allow a family member or a friend to talk to us like that. So why do we do it to ourselves?

One reason is that as humans, our complex brains do all sorts of things we aren't even aware of. *Cognitive dissonance* is a phenomenon that describes the discomfort we feel when our values and behaviors don't align. People like to be consistent, so our actions tend to be in sync with our beliefs and values. When they aren't, we make an effort to line them up again. For example, if we start to rack up victories and accomplishments but still view ourselves as flawed, worthless, incapable, or deficient, we pull the plug on our success to get rid of the dissonance. If it feels bad to fail, it feels even worse to succeed.[36]

Again, self-awareness is important, as is controlling the narrative in your head. If you are thinking negative thoughts, your brain is going to look for evidence of those things. If you are telling yourself that you don't deserve the life you want most, that's a problem because your brain will believe it.

The significant impact that our own words have on our minds and well-being is the subject of the book *Words*

---

36 Ellen Hendriksen, "Why Do We Self-Sabotage?" *Psychology Today,* October 10, 2017, https://www.psychologytoday.com/sg/blog/how-be-yourself/201710/why-do-we-self-sabotage?amp.

Can Change Your Brain by Dr. Andrew Newberg, a neuroscientist at Thomas Jefferson University, and Mark Robert Waldman, a communications expert. In the book, they state, "A single word has the power to influence the expression of genes that regulate physical and emotional stress." They also explain how thinking positive thoughts can change our reality. "By holding a positive and optimistic [word] in your mind, you stimulate frontal lobe activity," they write. "This area includes specific language centers that connect directly to the motor cortex responsible for moving you into action. And as our research has shown, the longer you concentrate on positive words, the more you begin to affect other areas of the brain."[37]

Newberg and Waldman say that if we sustain positive thoughts over time, our self-perception and perception of those around us begin to change. In other words, holding a positive view of ourselves helps train our brain to see the good in others and in the world around us. This grants us the ability to shape our reality and change the world for the better.

---

37 Lindsey Horton, "The Neuroscience behind Our Words," Business Relationship Management Institute, August 8, 2019, https://brm.institute/neuroscience-behind-words.

Many times, we learn our negative self-talk as children from the adults around us. The narratives we hear as children can stick with us unless we make a conscious effort to challenge and change it. For example, if you grew up hearing that wealthy people are jerks, it's possible that you subconsciously resist accumulating wealth because you don't want to be a greedy, selfish jerk.

But are all wealthy people greedy, selfish jerks? Of course not. Change the narrative. Tell yourself, instead, that you deserve abundance and wealth. Repeat it until you believe it. Then your brain will seek out opportunities to create wealth, and you will slowly change that negative self-talk into positive self-talk—and potentially increase your wealth.

Most of the time, our negative self-talk happens automatically; we don't really think about it. Psychiatrist, physician, and author Dr. Daniel Amen calls this type of self-talk ANTs: automatic negative thoughts.[38] Don't get eaten by ANTs! Again, make a conscious effort to change the narrative.

Doing this requires self-awareness. Pay attention to the way you talk to yourself. If much of your self-talk is negative, stop yourself right when you have a negative thought

---

38   Chris Winfield, "How to Stop Negative Thinking with 3 Easy Steps," *Inc.*, accessed February 9, 2022, https://www.inc.com/chris-winfield/is-stomping-ants-the-key-to-living-a-happier-life.html.

and replace it with a positive thought. If you continue to let negative thoughts run rampant through your mind, they will eat you alive.

In Chapter 4, we discussed how important it is to surround yourself with people who will encourage and support you. If you're having a bad day and feel like giving up, seek out some words of encouragement from the five people in your life who are closest to you. They can help you through the rough spots. Don't hesitate to reach out to them and tell them whatever you're going through. They will most likely be happy to help you; helping you probably makes them feel good.

CALM YOUR FEARS

Allowing fear to drive our decisions is another thing we do to get in our own way. We find that even wealthy people worry if they will have enough money to retire on. Some people are so worried about running out of money in retirement that they live like misers when they could actually afford to spend some money on themselves. They deny themselves the things they want because of this fear; they err on the side of caution.

It's great to be cautious, but it's no fun to live in retirement pinching pennies when it isn't necessary. This is another reason why it is helpful to team up with an advisor who can help you figure out just how much money you might need in retirement. It is wonderful when clients sit down with us and tell us what they would love to do, and then, when we put some numbers on paper, they realize they can do much more than they ever thought possible.

Instead of letting fear quash your dreams, just put your dreams out there and discuss them with your advisor. Ask if they might be possible. In our experience, there is almost always a way to make it work. With a little planning, we can help you save for the future while also enjoying your life. You don't have to choose one or the other.

We have had clients who thought they couldn't afford to take family trips, but when we looked at the numbers, those trips were absolutely possible. When they realized they could create wonderful memories with their families on those trips, they were so thankful that going forward, they began to speak up and say what they really wanted. If you never speak up—if you never put your dreams out there—you are less likely to get what you want out of life.

What's the worst that can happen? Not being able to afford a trip this year, maybe, or even the next. But if you work with your right-fit advisor, you can figure out *when* you will be able to take that trip. If you surround yourself with supportive people and gain access to effective financial planning but don't speak up about what you really want, those resources won't help you much. Be your own advocate for living your best life. Don't let fear drive the bus.

If you do not feel comfortable sharing your dreams with your financial advisor, you are working with the wrong financial advisor. This is why we push so much for people to engage with us during The Dream Architect™ planning process: if we can discover up front what you want most and get to the core of what motivates you, that helps us do our job better. We can design a financial plan for you, but unless you share what you really want out of life, we cannot help you live the life you really want.

That is why we created The Dream Architect™ process. We don't want people living their lives thinking, "What if...?" We want them to discover what they really love, and then we help them weigh their options.

LET THE PAST GO

We've seen people spend a lot of time and energy on the "if only" scenarios—looking back and wishing they had pursued something that fear kept them from pursuing.

This is counterproductive. There is absolutely nothing we can do about the past. We cannot change what has already happened. Extract the lesson from each situation and move forward. Everything that has happened in your life up to this point has brought you to where you are today. It is your starting point. If things that happened in your past make you sad, mad, and frustrated, don't spend any more energy on them. You cannot change them. What you *can* influence, though, is what happens in your future.

You have the opportunity to create the life you most want, and it boils down to a few key steps:

1. Decide what you want most in life—define your values.
2. Surround yourself with positive, uplifting people who push you to be the best version of yourself.
3. Pursue what you want most—say it out loud and discuss it with your financial advisor.
4. Be an uplifting, positive example to others.
5. Let go of what you cannot control and focus on what you can.

As the C. S. Lewis quote at the beginning of Chapter 2 says, "You can't go back and change the beginning, but you can start where you are and change the ending." And Dan Sullivan, The Strategic Coach, says, "The past is just as much a fiction as the future. You're the one making it up."

Get out of your own way. Push aside all those obstacles—excuses, fear, negative self-talk—and write the narrative that will guide you to your best possible future.

YOUR TOOLBOX FOR GETTING OUT OF YOUR OWN WAY

1. What types of negative self-talk have you notice yourself thinking or saying? In the left column of the chart below, write down several ways you put yourself down. Then, in the right column, change the narrative—write what you will tell yourself instead. We have provided an example to get you started.

My Usual Negative Self-Talk	What I Will Say Instead in the Future
What a stupid mistake! What is wrong with me?	I will do better next time.

2. What are some activities you have said yes to in the past that took time, energy, and focus away from your goals? These are activities you might consider saying no to in the future. List them below.

_____

_____

_____

_____

_____

CHAPTER 6

FIND YOUR WHOS

"Focus on who instead of how."

—DEAN JACKSON, FOUNDER, I LOVE MARKETING

With any endeavor in life, including retirement, people tend to get caught up in how they're going to accomplish something. From the little tasks to the big ones, people tend to spin their wheels trying to figure out "how am I going to get this done?"

If this tends to be your approach, we want you to start thinking differently, with more of a focus on who in your life can help you accomplish your goals, as opposed to how you can reach them alone.

In earlier chapters, we discussed the importance of surrounding yourself with people who will cheer you on and who want to see you live a fulfilled life versus holding you back and "shoulding" on you. Your right-fit financial advisor, for example, can likely be the most important who in your life when it comes to planning your financial future.

FOCUSING ON YOUR WHOS WILL INCREASE YOUR RESULTS

Dean Jackson, founder of I Love Marketing, originally stressed the importance of focusing on who instead of how. Dan Sullivan, founder of Strategic Coach®, coined his own specific concept, WhoNotHow: when you set out to accomplish a goal, ask yourself, "Who can get me there faster?" Focus on the aspects of that goal you excel at—the things you have energy and passion for—and delegate the other aspects to people who are really good at those tasks.

This idea is the focus of the 2020 book *Who Not How*. Entrepreneurial coach Dr. Benjamin Hardy wrote the book based on his interviews with Dan Sullivan. (In the book's dedication, the authors acknowledge and thank Dean Jackson for originating the term "who not how.") The authors state that by simply asking yourself "Who can do this for me?" when you set out to accomplish something, you will expand your abundance of wealth, innovation, relationships, and joy and build a life in which everything you do is your choice. "Your identity and purpose will expand as you have experiences of encouragement and support through the right Whos," they write. "Moreover, by getting certain Whos involved in your current goals and vision, that vision will expand and grow dramatically."[39]

The authors note that, alone, we can never accomplish as much as we can when we collaborate with others:

> Are you keeping your goals so small that you can accomplish them on your own? Do you really think you must be the one to put in the blood, sweat, and tears, shouldering the whole load to prove your capability? *Results*, not effort, is the name of the game. You are rewarded in life by the results you produce, not the effort and time you put in.[40]

Bryan considers this the most life-changing book he's read. He believes that if you read this book and take the

---

39 Dan Sullivan and Benjamin Hardy, *Who Not How: The Formula to Achieve Bigger Goals through Accelerating Teamwork* (Carlsbad, CA: Hay House Business, 2020), 174.

40 Sullivan and Hardy, *Who Not How*, 7.

principles to heart, it will have an amazing effect on your career and on your life.

RETIREMENT IS NOT A DIY PROJECT

No one excels at everything. Sometimes people are tempted to try the do-it-yourself, or DIY, approach to remodeling their homes or repairing their vehicles, whether it's to save money or to feel the satisfaction of accomplishing it. You might enjoy playing with your finances and trying to figure out how to maximize your money in retirement. But you haven't helped thousands of other people retire. You haven't gone through that process to see what works and what doesn't because there has been no "testing ground" for you. When you're doing it yourself, you have one chance. You have one retirement. Don't take a chance on something this important.

Some things in life are just fine to be DIY'd. But creating the life you can't wait to wake up to and allowing your money to work best for you is not one of those things.

You don't know what you don't know. Financial services products are complex, as are the tax laws. Financial advisors who have years of experience have navigated market downturns and other disruptive situations, such as the COVID-19 pandemic. Do you really want to spend your time and energy managing your finances? Do you want to try to figure out how to maximize your money in retirement by yourself, or do you want to work with someone who helps people retire every single day? And once you've retired, do you want to worry about your finances or spend more time with your grandkids and travel? The choice is yours.

Let your financial advisor—the person focused on aligning your dreams with your finances—do the worrying for you.

TIME IS FINITE—SPEND IT DOING THE THINGS YOU ENJOY

Time is the only thing in life you can't get more of. Use this finite resource wisely; optimize it by thoroughly enjoying everything you do. Delegate the things you don't enjoy or excel at to somebody who has that expertise. Doing this will make it easier for you to focus on your area of expertise, which in turn will make your journey to retirement much more enjoyable.

How many times have you missed out on an opportunity for self-improvement because you felt like you didn't have time for it? People will say or think things like, "I don't have time to read this motivational book or take this course that would help me because I need to mow the lawn." Why not pay someone who mows lawns for a living so you can take time to learn more important things for yourself?

Your life could improve significantly if you delegate some activities to other people. Imagine how much energy you would have for the things you love in life if you no longer had to worry about the things you don't enjoy.

Over the years, some of Bryan's fellow study group members[41] have teased him about delegating to other people the tasks he doesn't enjoy. But he is focused on doing the things he knows and is passionate about, which frees up his time and energy to be creative. It's much easier to be innovative when you are passionate about what you're doing.

It's true. The only things Bryan does are the things he thinks will improve his life. You have to prioritize things. Figure out what you want most in life and commit to spending your time doing those things. Since you can't make more hours, you have to give up something to get something.

When you engage in activities you don't enjoy and aren't good at, it's hard to muster the motivation to get started on them. That leads to procrastination. Rather than struggle with the how in the face of your own resistance to doing

---

41 Twice a year, Bryan meets with four like-minded financial advisors to help one another enhance their practices.

everything on your own, Dan Sullivan says that overall, the better question to ask is "Who?":[42]

- Who do you want to learn from?
- Who is already doing what you want to be doing?
- Who is where you want to be?
- Who fascinates and/or inspires you?
- Who do you want to collaborate with?
- Who do you want to help?

A lack of clarity about your goals causes procrastination, too. Having the right who in your life to help create this clarity will help you overcome procrastination about planning for the future.

HAVING A STRONG WHY WILL HELP YOU FIGURE OUT THE WHO

Dr. Benjamin Hardy and many other researchers stress that when your why—your reason for doing something—is strong enough, you will figure out the who.

---

42 Benjamin Hardy, "Want More Energy and Bigger Results? Stop Asking 'How' and Start Asking 'Who,'" BenjaminHardy.com, accessed February 9, 2022, https://benjaminhardy.com/want-more-energy-and-bigger-results-stop-asking-how-and-start-asking-who-2.

If you envision your retirement as being able to wake up every day with no agenda, no real purpose, then you probably won't care who handles your financial affairs or helps you plan for the future. But when you have a strong why—when you actually know what you want out of life and why—you will gain clarity about the type of financial advisor you want to work with.

If you want to live a dream-focused life and have a long bucket list, you probably want to work with an advisor who does more than basic investment management. You're going to want a wealth advisor who is experienced in helping people realize their greatest dreams to guide you. We help people retire well every day, and we are passionate about doing so.

BUSINESS OWNERS HAVE A UNIQUE SITUATION

Focusing on your strengths is especially important for business owners. We see many who devoted so much of their time and effort to their organizations that when it comes time to retire, they really can't do so because they have no identity outside their work. They are lost when they retire and don't have the business to focus on anymore.

If you hire people who excel in the areas you do not excel in, that will free up your time and energy to take your business to the next level. Focusing on your strengths and hiring people whose strengths complement yours will benefit you and your team.

Now, it costs money to hire team members or contractors to take care of tasks you prefer not to focus on. We recommend that you do a cost-benefit analysis to discover if it would benefit you to hire experts.

We'll use the legal field as an example. To quantify the returns on delegation, a team of researchers studied the law profession in which partners delegate legal work to associates. They analyzed data from thousands of law offices regarding how much partners make, how many associates work with them, and how much those associates and other staff cost the firm in salary and benefits. The researchers combined those data with an economic model to estimate how much lawyers benefit when they work with associates.[43]

They found that when partners delegated work to associates, it allowed the median partners to earn at least 20 percent more than they would otherwise. Top lawyers, who have the most skill to leverage, earned at least 50 percent

---

43   Thomas N. Hubbard, "Research: Delegating More Can Increase Your Earnings," *Harvard Business Review*, August 12, 2016, https://hbr.org/2016/08/research-delegating-more-can-increase-your-earnings.

more. Delegating work to associates allowed partners to serve more clients. Also, clients were willing to pay the lawyers more per hour when they spent less time on routine issues and more on complicated ones. The researchers noted that if you find yourself having to turn down work, that is a sign that you might not be delegating enough.[44]

This is wise advice for business owners in any profession.

The more efficient your business operations are and the more efficient you are as a leader, the better you will be able to create a confident future for those who work for you. When you hire people who are even better than you at various tasks, it's a double win—not only are you empowering your team, but you are also freeing up your time and energy.

Then, once it's time for you to think about retirement, you will already have the right people in the right seats on the bus, taking care of their individual areas of expertise. It will give you more confidence that your business will continue to thrive if you decide to reduce the number of hours you work or turn the business over to a successor.

We designed our Smarter Business program to help business owners shift their focus from running day-to-day operations to executing big-picture and high-impact financial strategies. To reach the financial freedom,

---

44   Hubbard, "Research."

growth, and opportunity that attracted you to build your own business in the first place, you must replace tactical, reactionary financial moves with goal-aligned, preemptive, and strategic ones.

It is especially important for you, as a business owner, to have a wealth advisor in your corner who will help you navigate uncertainties and inspire you to find activities outside your work to enjoy. Our Smarter Business program gives you access to tools and resources that will help you create a fulfilled life and get the right people in your corner to take care of all the tasks you do not want to focus on.

If something feels tedious, like a chore, and if it saps your energy, that is a great indication that it's a task you don't enjoy. Delegate it.

WHY PEOPLE RESIST SEEKING HELP

This concept is simple and powerful: delegate the tasks you aren't good at and don't enjoy to people who do excel in them. So why don't more people focus on the who, as opposed to the how, when planning their retirement or reaching other important goals?

Dr. Benjamin Hardy says one reason people don't seek out experts to help them is because no one teaches us this important concept:

The public school-system does not teach people to become WHO-thinkers and collaborators. Instead, the school system teaches people how to become HOW-thinkers, equipped with a seemingly endless amount of generalized skillsets.

Rather than looking for *others* to work with, kids are taught to compete against others and look for right answers. There is basically zero training on developing mentorships, collaborations, partnerships, teamwork, and leadership. Even as a PhD student, I've been surprised how generalized my education has been. Rather than working with specific WHO's, my whole education has been a non-stop flow of HOW's.[45]

Another reason people often resist seeking help is because it typically costs money to hire professionals. However, it pays to review how a professional could save you more money than the money you spend to hire him or her. For example, what if your wealth advisor found hundreds of thousands of dollars in tax savings for you over your lifetime? That's going to cover the cost of trying to do it yourself many times over.

Again, you don't know what you don't know. Do a cost-benefit analysis to figure out how it could benefit

---

45   Hardy, "Want More Energy and Bigger Results?"

you to hire a professional. Be aware of the ways in which you might leave money on the table by building your own retirement plan.

Few people are as committed to their financial futures on their own as they would be if they had a wealth planner advising them. One in five people, 20 percent, spend more time planning for a family vacation than they do planning their finances.[46] Again, you have just one opportunity to retire well, so it makes sense to hire professionals to help you make the most of your hard-earned money and plan for the future.

We see many people who have made few or no preparations when they reach retirement. They suddenly realize there was so much more they could have done in the years leading up to retirement that would have enhanced their ability to enjoy that next phase of life. They have regrets about putting their heads in the sand all those years. The best way to avoid having regrets is to be proactive about your retirement. Hire a wealth advisor to guide you.

In the financial world, people talk a lot about their "return on investment." We prefer to focus on a "return on

---

46   Mallika Mitra, "You're Not Alone if You Spend More Time Planning Your Vacation than Working on Your Finances," CNBC, August 2, 2019, https://www.cnbc.com/2019/08/02/1-in-5-people-spend-more-time-planning-vacations-than-finances-survey.html.

life." Your finances are just the *avenue* to your best life; they are not your *purpose* in life.

IT'S NEVER TOO LATE TO START

Having the right who in your corner is particularly important for women in transition. About 50 percent of all marriages end in divorce, and the average age of a widow is fifty-eight and a half.[47]

Many women we work with have never been involved with their finances. When their husbands pass away, or when they get divorced, they don't know where to begin to get their finances in order. This is stressful for them. We remind them that they don't need all the answers; they just need the right people in their corner to help them figure it out based on what their dreams are.

When you are juggling many roles in life and taking care of other people, it can be overwhelming if suddenly you have to manage your finances, too. That's why someone who implements The Dream Architect™ process can be so valuable. That person becomes a huge ally in your life.

---

47   Whitney Amann, "Health Living: Modern Widow," 9&10 News, September 30, 2019, https://www.9and10news.com/2019/09/30/healthy-living-modern-widow.

Our Women Forward program encourages women to take charge of their wealth, make empowered and confident decisions, and pursue their biggest dreams—even if they've evolved unexpectedly over time.

In some of our Women Forward sessions, when we discuss planning for retirement, women will say, "Well, I'm too old for that." Brittany's rebuttal to that is always, "Okay, check your behind. Do you have an expiration date on there? No." We don't know when our time is up, so she doesn't believe you're ever too old or too young to pursue what you want most.

Another response we have to this comment is, "Well, how old will you be next year?" If someone says, "I'll be seventy," then we'll say, "Whether you do this planning or not, you are still going to be seventy. So why not go ahead and do it?" You're going to be that age, no matter what. Plus, you're younger now than you'll ever be again.

GRATITUDE AND HOBBIES
IMPROVE YOUR WELL-BEING

When Bryan's aunt Jean was ninety years old, Brittany did an interview with her because she used the *Imagine. Act. Inspire.* journal that Bryan and Brittany created. Jean used it every day. She read the inspirational quotes, wrote down her three top activities for the day, and wrote who and what she was grateful for. She even wrote notes in the margins.

It was inspiring to Brittany to hear Jean talk about how grateful she was for her friendships and her home and how she was excited about taking a painting class simply because she enjoyed painting. Brittany thought, *If she can commit to focusing on the things she loves at ninety years old, then anybody can. So there's no excuse not to.*

Jean was a testament to how rewarding it is when people design the life they want. Instead of worrying about money, they can focus on what they are grateful for and what energizes them. Focusing on those things every day will give you energy and excitement, which can help keep you sharp, healthy, and excited about the future.

One study showed that people who kept an online gratitude journal for two weeks reported better physical health, including fewer headaches, less stomach pain, clearer skin, and reduced congestion.[48]

An article in *Psychology Today* reported that people who engage in mental activities tend to have better memory and executive functioning skills and a reduced risk of

---

48 Emiliana R. Simon-Thomas, "A 'Thnx' a Day Keeps the Doctor Away," *Greater Good Magazine*, December 19, 2012, https://greatergood.berkeley. edu/article/item/a_thnx_a_day_keeps_the_doctor_away.

dementia. Examples of beneficial activities include reading, playing a musical instrument or singing, doing crossword puzzles, drawing or painting, taking community courses, playing board games or cards, or going to museums. Many of these activities are free or inexpensive and readily available.[49]

It's a wonderful cycle: if you have professionals help you plan your financial future, you will free up time and energy to do the things you love, which can improve your well-being as you enter retirement.

HOW TO FIND THE RIGHT WHO TO GUIDE YOU TO RETIREMENT

One of the reasons many people come on board with us at Sweet Financial Partners is that they don't hear regularly from their current advisors. Because life is dynamic, it's important for your advisor to work closely with you on an ongoing basis to determine if any adjustments need to be made to your retirement plan. Too many times, people fail to make the necessary adjustments to their plans when

---

49 John Randolph, "The Benefits of Brain-Boosting Hobbies," *Psychology Today*, April 9, 2020, https://www.psychologytoday.com/us/blog/the-healthy-engaged-brain/202004/the-benefits-brain-boosting-hobbies.

they get married or divorced, have children or grandchildren, or buy or a sell a business. If you have a financial advisor but are still wondering if you'll be okay in retirement, then why not seek out a second opinion?

Look for a team or a company that operates in a way that resonates with you and what you want to accomplish. At Sweet Financial Partners, we believe a positive, dream-focused mindset is the foundation for a sound retirement. This incredible phase of your life is about so much more than just the amount of money you have saved.

We practice what we teach and preach. If you come into our office, you're going to see images of our clients' dreams and what matters most to them. You'll also see our team's dream board, where we post visual representations of what we want to manifest in our lives. You will see that everyone here is rooting for our clients to have the best possible future.

NEXT STEPS

Seek out professionals to guide you to retirement. You will be grateful you did. Michael Fishman, an entrepreneur in healthcare, says, "Self-made is an illusion. There are many people who play divine roles in you having a life that you have today. Be sure to let them know how grateful you are."

YOUR TOOLBOX FOR
FINDING YOUR WHOS

1. Below, list some areas of your life that you have tried to handle on your own but are not your area of expertise and you don't enjoy.

_____

_____

_____

_____

2. Now list experts in those areas to whom you can turn those tasks over so you can focus on the activities you excel at and enjoy.

_____

_____

_____

_____

Your financial advisor is likely the most important who in your life when it comes to planning your financial future. Whether you have a financial advisor, visit *www.sweetchecklist.com* to download our Wealth Confidence Checklist. Complete the ten-question checklist to determine if your advisor is the best guide to helping you design the retirement you can't wait to wake up to.

CHAPTER 7

NAVIGATING UNCERTAINTY AND ADVERSITY

"Happiness can be found even in the darkest of times, if one only remembers to turn on the light."

—ALBUS DUMBLEDORE

Being optimistic, staying positive, and dreaming big isn't all woo-woo stuff. We don't recommend a positive mindset just because it creates a feel-good, warm-fuzzy feeling. There's really a purpose to it. Part of that purpose is that when you have a plan for what your dream life looks like, it helps you hold to a higher vision during times of uncertainty and adversity.

We're not saying you will never feel down, but staying focused on the positive will help you avoid *staying* down.

We are writing this book right in the middle of the COVID-19 pandemic. It is proof that adversity will come at some point for all of us. Regarding your finances, there are some things you can do to prepare for downturns, such as diversifying your portfolio to spread your risk among various types of investments. But in general, we just have to live our lives the best we can during the ups and downs and know that the tide will turn. The people who hold true to a future vision and to their big-picture, long-term plans are the ones who tend to remain calm and focused during tumultuous times. They understand that they're in it for the long game, so the temporary glitches don't throw them off course.

Remember when we told you about Sean Stephenson in Chapter 1? He was born with a rare disease that stunted his growth and caused pain and hundreds of broken bones over his lifetime. When he died after a fall at the age of forty, his last words were, "This is happening *for* me, not *to* me." When we face difficult situations—which we always will—we all could benefit from the mindset Sean had: things happen *for* us, not *to* us. When circumstances are beyond our control, we cannot change the situation; we can only change the way we respond to it.

Some people say everything happens for a reason, as if every event stems naturally from the past. We're not sure that's true because some really bad things happen randomly to amazing people, but we do think we can find a *purpose* from all of it. Look for the lesson, for any type of positive outcome, that can emerge from a negative situation. What can you learn from it moving forward?

Staying positive during difficult times doesn't make you naive; it just helps you realize that regardless of what happens, you're going to be okay. When you keep your focus on your long-term goals, it can help you get through the tough times.

Also, a positive mindset can benefit your physical health. According to Johns Hopkins University, people with a family history of heart disease who also had a positive outlook were one-third less likely to have a heart attack or other cardiovascular event within five to twenty-five years than those with a more negative outlook. Additional studies have found that a positive attitude improves outcomes and life satisfaction across a spectrum of conditions, including traumatic brain injury, stroke, and brain tumors.[50]

---

50   "The Power of Positive Thinking," Johns Hopkins Medicine, accessed February 9, 2022, https://www.hopkinsmedicine.org/health/wellness-and-prevention/the-power-of-positive-thinking.

GRATITUDE HELPS US NAVIGATE ADVERSITY, TOO

We have mentioned gratitude in previous chapters, and it's worth mentioning again here.

Expressing gratitude helps us cope with sadness, frustration, and anxiety. If you focus on what you're most grateful for, it makes it really hard to stay in a negative slump. In 2020, when we asked people what they were grateful for, nine times out of ten, they said they were grateful for their health and for the health of their loved ones. When all seems lost, we can always find something to be grateful for.

Many studies have proven the health benefits associated with a focus on gratitude. For example, Dr. Martin E. P. Seligman, a psychologist at the University of Pennsylvania, tested the impact of various positive psychology interventions on 411 people, each compared with a control assignment of writing about early memories. When their week's assignment was to write and personally deliver letters of gratitude to people who had never been properly thanked for their kindness, participants immediately exhibited a huge increase in happiness scores. This impact was greater than that from any other intervention, with benefits lasting for a month.[51]

---

51   "Giving Thanks Can Make You Happier," Harvard Medical School,...

Sometimes it helps just to look at things from a different angle. When dark times happen, that's when people feel like quitting or giving up. We believe the secret to persevering through those times is to keep hanging in there and taking even small actions to move forward and get through them. Just writing in a journal, reciting affirmations, and expressing gratitude can be helpful.

NOTICE WHEN YOU ARE FIXATING ON THE NEGATIVE

We are not saying that you can never be pessimistic; that's not realistic. Sometimes we don't even realize that we are fixating on a negative situation. When you notice yourself getting into a negative mindset and feeling discouraged about what's going on in the world around you, *recognize* that you are feeling that way. Then you can refocus and redirect your thoughts. Follow Lolly Daskal's advice: "You always have a choice: you can control your mind, or you can let it control you."

Sometimes we have to get comfortable with being uncomfortable. Even the most positive, upbeat people feel discouraged sometimes. Like everyone else, they have

---

...accessed January 27, 2022, https://www.health.harvard.edu/healthbeat/giving-thanks-can-make-you-happier.

to *choose* to focus on the possibilities that can arise from adversity and uncertainty, even as they're feeling low. No one wakes up feeling great every single day.

We must control our mindset and actions and be intentional about the way we react to a situation versus letting life knock you down and keep you down.

HAVE AN ALLY SAY A TRIGGER WORD TO YOU

When you're in the belly of the negativity beast, it can be difficult to look at your situation with perspective and recognize that you need to emerge from it. Someone else might need to help you realize you are wallowing in negativity. But it can be difficult for people to try to pull someone from a downward spiral when they are in the depths of it.

In those situations, it can help to have the people closest to you say a pre-established "trigger word" to snap you out of your negative funk.

In the 2004 comedy *Meet the Fockers*, Dina Byrnes, played by Blythe Danner, speaks the word "muskrat" when she wants her high-strung husband, former CIA operative Jack Byrnes, played by Robert DeNiro, to lighten up. Although that's a movie, in reality, trigger words really work.

Come up with a word now and share it with your inner circle. Ask them to say that word to you when they see you headed down the rabbit hole of negativity. Get yourself a "muskrat"!

SOMETIMES WE NEED A BATTERY RECHARGE

Sometimes we need a change of scenery or a change of pace to break free from negativity—a battery recharge. Genius marketers Dean Jackson and Joe Polish talk about having Super Happy Fun Days. When the prevailing mood is gloomy, they schedule a lot of fun things for one day—activities that make them feel positive and happy. They are intentional about focusing on fun and positivity, whether it's once a month, a couple of times a month, or once a quarter.

When you feel stressed or down, you might just need to have your cup filled back up. It doesn't matter if the cup is half empty or half full; what matters is that it can be filled. Why not schedule something fun for yourself to rejuvenate your spirit and give your mind a break? It doesn't have to be a big extravagant trip or event. Just be intentional about setting aside some fun time for yourself. It will help you stay focused on the good stuff.

Maybe you are feeling so distraught about something that it's impossible to focus on your priorities in the moment. Do something fun *right then* to change your mental focus. Be proactive about changing your mood—don't worry about planning it in advance. Too many times, people give up when they are so close to the finish line. If they had just stayed with it a little longer, they could have overcome the obstacles they were facing.

Do whatever it takes to give yourself a little boost, some inspiration. Here are twelve suggestions of small actions you can take to feel better right now:

1. Write in your journal.
2. List five things you are grateful for.
3. Take a drive.
4. Take a walk.
5. Visit a park—being surrounded by nature can calm your mood.
6. Listen to upbeat music.
7. Watch a funny video clip, show, or movie.
8. Read something just for fun, not work related.
9. Call a positive, supportive person for a boost.
10. Plan something fun so you have something to look forward to.
11. Make someone or something better—volunteer your time to help somebody less fortunate than you, or pay for the coffee for the person behind you.
12. Clear out some clutter in your home or office.

Don't fall victim to your circumstances! Bad things happen to good people all the time. What matters is how you deal with those situations. Look for purpose or a potential lesson during those times of adversity. Ask yourself, "What is this teaching me?" or "What can I learn from this?" Many adverse situations you overcome will prepare you even more for situations that might arise in the future.

We are not saying you have to be grateful when something bad happens. But try to find the positive by-products or aftereffects of a situation. We help many people navigate some of the biggest transitions in life, including retirement, loss of a spouse, and a spouse being diagnosed with dementia or another debilitating illness. Life has a way of throwing curveballs at us, so we need to be equipped with great planning and sources of support, whether internal or external.

Now, we have stated how important it is to surround yourself with positive, supportive people. However, we cannot expect that other people will help us out of every negative situation. We must build up our stores of perseverance and resilience.

Seek support from others, but don't let other people become your only source of support. Are you trying to get somebody else's approval or waiting for someone else to tell you which way to go in life? Many people look outside themselves to have something or someone else make them happy. Instead, be your own source of happiness.

Napoleon Hill, the author of *Think and Grow Rich*, said, "It takes half your life before you discover life is a do-it-yourself project."

TRANSFORM NEGATIVE EXPERIENCES INTO POSITIVE ONES

Dan Sullivan, co-founder of Strategic Coach®, developed an exercise he calls The Experience Transformer®. The essence of it is that when something happens to you in your business or life in general, whether it seems "good" or "bad" to you in the moment, ask yourself three questions:

1. What worked?
2. What didn't work?
3. If I could do this over from scratch, how could I do it better?

Sullivan says that by finding better ways to progress, you introduce multipliers of investment and effort that then produce different results in the future.[52]

---

52   Dan Sullivan, "Transforming Experiences into Multipliers," The...

You don't know what you don't know. But by asking yourself these questions, you hopefully will discover truths that can lead to a life-changing occurrence.

As we sit here writing this book in the middle of the COVID-19 pandemic, the times we are facing now are actually a great example of how to use Sullivan's premise. If you were to sit and reflect on all the challenges that 2020 has presented and only focus on the negative, it could very well seem like a downright rotten year.

Simply reframing your thoughts with The Experience Transformer methodology can completely shift your thinking in a positive way. Rather than thinking about the frustrations, uncertainties, and challenges before you, instead focus on what went right in 2020. Maybe you got to spend additional time at home with your family that you wouldn't have had otherwise. Maybe you own a business and were able to completely innovate how you serve your clients or the services you offer. Maybe you have small children at home and you survived distance learning.

Now, take the thought one step further and say, "If I could go back and repeat 2020, without being able to change what

...Multiplier Mindset Blog, Strategic Coach, accessed January 27, 2022, https://resources.strategiccoach.com/the-multiplier-mindset-blog/ transforming-experiences-into-multipliers.

happened but rather how I responded to it, what could have been better, and how would that have been different?" That question is chock-full of opportunities for growth.

If you apply this methodology to your life, think about how truly monumental it can be—not only in terms of how you respond to tough situations but also in terms of how it will help you be a model for others to see how strong you stand in the face of adversity.

A METHOD FOR REFRAMING A MISTAKE IN A POSITIVE WAY

Here's an example of how we can help our clients reframe what might seem like a mistake as a positive, using the Dan Sullivan Experience Transformer method.

Let's say we have a new client who had made a hasty decision to retire early without first seeking the insight of his advisor. It was an in-the-moment decision that, going forward without proper planning, could have truly devastated his plans for the future. The biggest mistake was not leaning more on an advisor as an expert resource before making such a big decision. The good news is that this client could meet with us, and we would be able to course correct and help ensure that he makes informed decisions going forward that would positively impact his plan.

By starting with the question of "What went right?" we can see just how important early retirement was for this person's mental well-being. He was reaching a point of burnout in his existing position, and he felt liberated by making this decision for himself and his family.

We would then navigate to the question of "What didn't go so right?" This can be a difficult question because it requires real introspection to give an honest answer. In this case, the early retiree is now uncertain if he can accomplish everything he wants in retirement, even by cutting his income a little short. So what didn't go right was that he didn't start his plan early enough, and he made a decision without relying first on his trusted advisor.

Next, by quickly navigating into the solution phase, we can ask, "What steps can be put in place to help turn this into a positive?" Then we can make proper adjustments to this person's plan and help give him a new roadmap to follow. Our goal is always to help people see the *possibility* in their future, even if that future is a little different than initially envisioned. Maybe, in this case, the early retiree has another passion he wants to pursue that could create additional income to help offset the early retirement. Maybe through some minor spending adjustments and reprioritizing, he can still accomplish the most important things and be able to enjoy the rest of what life has to offer.

As you can see, by actively searching for the good in a given situation, it is so much easier to see possibilities rather than failure.

DO SOMETHING THAT
PRODUCES VISIBLE RESULTS

One time, a colleague of ours in the financial services industry was talking about golf. He said, "The reason I like golf so much is because in my business, you can't always measure improvement directly because you're always going forward and the target is always changing. But in golf, you can measure your improvement exactly."

Brittany thinks that's an interesting thought process. That's why she enjoys repurposing old furniture or taking a room or space that looked cluttered or shabby before and redesigning it into something beautiful. With activities like these, you can track progress and see the finish line.

If you are a business owner or you're in a high-profile career, it can be difficult to weather adversity and uncertainty if you're always on the hamster wheel and unable to see a finish line. Constantly moving without seeing results can cause a negative mental state. But if you have an outside pursuit that allows you to see tangible progress, that's a great way to stay positive. If you don't have an activity like this right now, find one you enjoy. Use it as a fallback or a go-to when you're feeling discouraged.

ACCEPT WHEN YOU CANNOT CONTROL A SITUATION

During those times in life when we face situations we cannot control, it is futile to try to do so. Many people spin their wheels, trying to influence situations that are beyond their control. They spend too much mental and emotional energy trying to change things they cannot change. A much better approach is simply to let go, accept the circumstances, and figure out how to get through them.

When you are faced with a distressing situation, ask yourself, "Is this within my control?" When the answer is yes, do what you can to make things better. But if the answer is no, then quit worrying about it because there's nothing you can do.

REVISIT YOUR VALUES

As we've mentioned before, it helps to stop sometimes and revisit your values. When you are clear about what you want for the future, it makes it easier to endure uncertainty and adversity. You are focused on the future, not on the current circumstances.

Another helpful strategy is to ask yourself, "Is this going to matter in five years?" If the answer is no, stop stressing about it. Follow the "five-by-five rule," which says, "If it won't matter in five years, don't spend more than five minutes worrying about it."

DON'T LET MARKET DOWNTURNS ALTER YOUR LONG-TERM PATH

We have noticed that people who have embraced a long-term, dream-focused mindset are able to keep their eyes on what truly matters, even during adversity. This is why we believe so strongly in the value of The Dream Architect™ process because it can help mitigate uncertainty by focusing on long-term goals.

Those who do not have a strong vision and clear values are more likely to get tossed about in the storms of life. When people get too caught up in negativity, reacting sharply to immediate problems, they often make short-term decisions that adversely affect their long-term goals.

For example, during market downturns, some people panic and pull out of the market instead of riding out the situation and staying focused on their long-term goals. Studies have shown that this is a losing strategy. You are typically better off riding out a market downturn than you are pulling out of the market.

According to Investopedia,

In down markets, investors are understandably often overcome by their "loss aversion" instincts, thinking that if they don't sell, they stand to lose more money. However, the decline of the asset's value is often temporary and will go back up. On the other hand, if the investor sells when the market is down, they will realize a loss. A lesson many investors have learned is that even though it can be challenging to watch a declining market—and not pull out—it is worth it to sit tight and wait for the upturn to come.[53]

J. P. Morgan's "Guide to Retirement™: 2019 Edition" notes that an investor with $10,000 in the S&P 500 index who stayed fully invested between January 4, 1999 and December 31, 2018 would have about $30,000. An investor

---

53   Richard Best, "3 Reasons Not to Sell after a Market Downturn," Investopedia, last modified August 30, 2021, https://www.investopedia. com/articles/investing/021116/3-reasons-not-sell-after-market-downturn. asp#citation-1.

who missed ten of the best days in the market would have under $15,000. A very skittish investor who missed thirty of the best days would have less than what they started with—$6,213, to be exact.[54]

When we do come across nervous Nellie clients who are tempted to pull out of the market at the first sign of a downturn, through The Dream Architect™ process we are typically able to remind them of their long-term goals, talk sense into them, and convince them to keep their portfolios intact.

Instead of letting negative news or poor advice tempt you into making sudden decisions based on short-term fluctuations, focus instead on your dreams, your long-term goals, and the things you've told us are most important to you. Enjoy life because it won't last forever. We get only one go-around.

---

54 "Guide to Retirement™: 2019 Edition," J. P. Morgan, https://www. amgchico.com/pdf/2019%20guide%20to%20retirement.pdf. For illustrative purposes only and does not represent any specific portfolio or any particular investment. The information provided is based on a hypothetical $10,000 investment in the indexes shown as of the stated dates. Indexes are unmanaged, do not reflect the deduction of fees or expenses, and are not available for direct investment. Dividends are not guaranteed and may be increased, decreased, or suspended altogether at the discretion of the issuing company. Past performance is not a reliable indicator or guarantee of future results.

YOUR LEGACY DEPENDS ON STAYING THE COURSE

In the grand scheme of things, a market downturn is one moment in the course of history. It will impact us for a short time. And again, if you can't control a situation, such as a downturn, don't spend time and energy worrying about it.

Banksy once said, "They say you die twice—one time when you stop breathing and a second time, a bit later on, when somebody says your name for the last time." The legacy you want to leave may depend on staying the course. If you focus only on the bad news in the world at any given time, that is not staying true to the legacy you want to leave behind, especially if you let that bad news sway your decision-making process. Your bigger purpose matters. How you think, how you behave, and what you put out into the world truly matter.

Time is one of the only things in this world that you can't get more of. If you're wasting time worrying about things that are beyond your control, that's insanity. The quicker you can pull out of that, the better.

Bryan once saw a compelling demonstration of life's brevity at a conference presentation. There used to be yardsticks that had six one-foot sections and they folded out, and a presenter was using one to emphasize the amount of time we have left. He unfolded the yardstick all the way out and began to break pieces off. At the end, he held up a small piece and said, "This is all the time you have left. Do you want to use it for positive, uplifting things, or do you want to sit and worry about everything beyond your control?"

When you realize how precious time is and how little of it is left, you want to make every day a darn good day.

SMILE TO TRICK YOUR BRAIN INTO THINKING YOU'RE HAPPY

When you're feeling down, depressed, anxious, and pessimistic, the last thing you want to do is smile. But did you know that if you smile, it will trick your brain into thinking you are happy? And that spurs actual feelings of happiness.

Science has shown that the mere act of smiling can lift your mood, lower stress, boost your immune system, and possibly even prolong your life. Dr. Murray Grossan, an otolaryngologist in Los Angeles, says, "What's crazy is that just the physical act of smiling can make a difference in building your immunity. When you smile, the brain 'sees' the muscle [activity] and assumes that humor is happening."[55]

55 Nicole Spector, "Smiling Can Trick Your Brain into Happiness—and Boost Your Health," NBC News, November 28, 2017, https://www.nbcnews.com/better/health/smiling-can-trick-your-brain-happiness-boost-your-health-ncna822591.

Your brain doesn't bother to sort out whether you're smiling because you're genuinely joyous or because you're just pretending. Dr. Sivan Finkel, a cosmetic dentist at New York City's The Dental Parlour, says, "Even forcing a fake smile can legitimately reduce stress and lower your heart rate." He adds, "A study performed by a group at the University of Cardiff in Wales found that people who could not frown due to Botox injections were happier on average than those who could frown."[56]

Now, we're not suggesting that you get Botox injections. But we are advocating for smiling, even when you don't feel like it—*especially* when you don't feel like it.

If you smile at other people, they'll smile back. It's contagious. And if you encourage someone else to smile, you've just made *them* feel better. Plus, it takes fewer muscles to smile than it does to frown.

GIVE YOURSELF SOMETHING TO LOOK FORWARD TO

When the world around you is filled with gloom and doom, it's easy to get caught up in that and feel trapped in your present circumstances. One way to encourage yourself to

---

56   Spector, "Smiling Can Trick."

look beyond the present is to give yourself something to look forward to, like a vacation.

There is evidence that certain forms of anticipation can reduce stress and anxiety. A 2015 study in the *Journal of Experimental Social Psychology* found that anticipating a positive event bolsters our mood and helps us endure a stressful task or event. Christian Waugh, coauthor of the study and an associate professor of psychology at Wake Forest University, writes, "Having things to look forward to is a major coping strategy. It helps us recover and adapt to stressors."

Waugh explains that the human brain can focus on only a couple of things at a time. "When you have positive, anticipatory things in your mind, there's just less room for negative thoughts," he says. "There's an overall better profile of positive to negative."[57]

So if you plan a vacation that gets you excited, it will help you feel optimistic during the tough times.

But again, as we've mentioned, the vacation or other event you plan doesn't have to be an elaborate, expensive trip around the world. You don't have to build a school for

57   Samuel S. Monfort, Hannah E. Stroup, and Christian Waugh, "The Impact of Anticipating Positive Events on Responses to Stress," *Journal of Experimental Social Psychology* 58 (2015): 11–22, https://doi.org/10.1016/j.jesp.2014.12.003.

children on the other side of the globe. It can be as simple as spending some time with your loved ones, going fishing, or lying on the beach.

Pursuing your dreams is like that, only on a much bigger scale. This is why we tell people, "We know what you're retiring *from*—your everyday job—but what are you retiring to? What is going to keep your cup full?"

We mentioned vision boards earlier. These are fun to put together, and they keep images of your dreams in front of you all the time. Seeing a picture or a written description of your dreams multiple times a day will encourage your brain to automatically work on ways to help you achieve them. Create a habit of focusing on what you want.

You'll get unsatisfyingly random results if you do random things. Be intentional about letting your dreams rise to the top of your consciousness, above and beyond the noise of negative news. Have a clear picture of your dreams so your brain can tell you how to get there.

YOUR DREAMS WILL CHANGE OVER TIME

Think about the dorm room or apartment you lived in when you first went out on your own. That space is no longer ideal or even adequate once you get married and have children. The same is true of the car you started out with. As we grow and evolve, our dreams change, too.

What motivated you twenty years ago might not motivate you now. And that's okay. You can change your goals and objectives at any time. Pursue whatever pushes you to be the best version of yourself now, even if that looks different than it did last year or five years ago.

This is why it's important to have a financial advisor who checks in with you regularly, not just once a year or even less often. When your life trajectory changes and you navigate major transitions, it can change your financial picture. Make sure your financial advisor is with you on your journey as your needs and dreams change.

YOUR TOOLBOX FOR NAVIGATING ADVERSITY AND UNCERTAINTY

1. Plan something to look forward to. To help you look past negative news, adversity, and uncertainty, plan something fun to do in the near future. Anticipating this will boost your

mood. What will you plan? Use the space below to write down some ideas.

_____

_____

_____

2. Think about an instance in your life (or business, if you're a business owner) where you wish the outcome could have been different. Following the exercise we mentioned earlier in this chapter, ask yourself:

a. What worked?

_____

_____

b. What didn't work?

_____

_____

c. What could I do to help this go better next time?

_____

_____

3. Use the framework above to work through every
   scenario where you either would have hoped
   for a different result or wanted the result to be
   even better next time.

CHAPTER 8

CONFIDENCE IS KEY

"With realization of one's own potential
and self-confidence in one's ability,
one can build a better world."

—Dalai Lama

When you have a plan for the future—a dream you're aiming for that's bigger than yourself, a possibility that you can hardly fathom for your life because it's so exceptional—it can build your confidence. As you make progress, you will feel a sense of achievement, which will further energize the pursuit of your goal.

People often think that the people who win are those with confidence. But we think it's the other way around— winning builds confidence and creates confident people.

When we meet many people for the first time, they understand that *financial* goals are important, but they do not always realize how important *life* goals are. The component many of them miss is that they are not setting targets for the future. They focus only on the numbers and fail to realize the why—the larger purpose—behind what they want to accomplish. And that's the most exciting part. If you plan your best future and then do the math backward from that prospective moment of achievement, you will discover how you can get to your most fulfilling life.

Using The Dream Architect™ process, we help people focus on their dreams and possibilities first and *then* figure out the numbers. As we've mentioned, people often know what they're retiring *from*, but many haven't yet figured out what they're retiring *to*.

HAVE SOMETHING EXCITING TO LOOK FORWARD TO

Without a compelling purpose to energize you and help you look forward to the future, retirement can seem like a yawning chasm of free time. That can be fun at first—getting up in the morning, not having to rush off to a job, watching *Wheel of Fortune*—but after a while, the novelty of free time will wear off, and it's likely that you will feel unfulfilled. That can lead to depression and even cognitive decline in many people. We have seen people deteriorate mentally and physically when they retire because they no longer feel useful, productive, or vibrant.

A 2017 study found that people who transitioned into retirement had worse overall functioning than those who continued to work. And they experienced double the rate of cognitive decline for working people of the same ages.[58]

During the COVID-19 pandemic, many people who were close to retirement age figured that maybe they should just retire early. But that is not the best decision in many cases.

Early retirement can mean significant, unanticipated healthcare costs, which become the biggest expense for most Americans as they age. You generally cannot get Medicare benefits before age sixty-five, and private health insurance can add the burden of tens of thousands of dollars to your expenses. The skyrocketing costs of long-term care can make working for another year or two financially prudent.

A May 2020 report from the New School's Retirement Equity Lab shows how the pandemic has eroded many

58   Sean A. P. Clouston and Nicole Denier, "Mental Retirement and Health Selection: Analyses from the US Health and Retirement Study," *Social Science & Medicine* 178 (2017): 78–86, https://doi.org/10.1016/j.socscimed.2017.01.019.

older employees' savings. The report says about three million more older workers will fall into lifelong poverty than otherwise would have without a coronavirus recession. Also, average retirement savings at age sixty-five for those with retirement assets were projected to drop by 31 percent post-recession.[59]

FOCUS ON ONE PRIORITY

We recently attended a training by Dr. Benjamin P. Hardy. He talked about how important it is to focus on one single outcome and then devote all your energy to that outcome you want for your life.

If you're a business owner, what does that look like to you? Does it mean you will select a successor and step back from some of the day-to-day operations? Does it mean you will sell a portion of your business? Or do you want to get out of the business completely right away? If you are a woman in transition who has gotten divorced or

---

59   Michael Papadopoulos et al., "Recession Increases Downward Mobility in Retirement: Middle Earners Hit from Both Sides," *Status of Older Workers Report* Series, Schwartz Center for Economic Policy Analysis at The New School for Social Research, May 2020, https://www.economicpolicyresearch.org/images/Retirement_Project/status_of_older_workers_reports/Q1_2020_OWAG_Final_2.pdf.

lost your husband, what does that one priority look like for you? And if you are about to retire, what is your one area of focus?

For many of the clients we work with, *family* is that one priority they want to focus on in retirement. They envision spending time with multiple generations and strengthening those bonds they weren't able to form while they were focused on their careers. They want to host reunions, vacations, and holiday events for their extended families to participate in.

What is more important to *you* than anything else?

DREAM FIRST, THEN PLAN

One way to build confidence is to recognize and celebrate even small wins.

People often underestimate what they can accomplish because they don't have anyone to show them the physical evidence of how their decisions impact their plan. It's hard to celebrate milestones when you have no target—or a fuzzy, out-of-focus target.

We mentioned in the beginning of this book that the proper mindset is critical to building the retirement you can't wait to wake up to. It's much more than just saving money. When you are clear about what you want to accomplish and every action you take aligns with that vision, you will be able to save for the future with more diligence and passion.

You can't measure your progress if you don't know where you're going.

When people start winding down their careers as they near retirement, they typically have a lot of questions: "If we move into a new house, how will that impact our future? If we go on this dream vacation, how will that affect our plan? If we commit to the charitable contributions we have always wanted to do, will that negatively impact our own retirement?"

As financial advisors, if we don't know what your goals are, we cannot answer those questions. We also cannot measure your progress. In turn, it will be hard for you to gain confidence about having an exciting, fulfilling future. That's why the dreaming has to come first, followed by the planning.

Once you figure out exactly what you want, then you can plan for it, and then the progress you make will build your confidence.

CELEBRATE EVEN THE SMALL WINS

Lofty goals are exhilarating, but they also can be overwhelming. Many people are hard on themselves. They don't allow themselves to appreciate their progress unless they've achieved something huge. That approach will not build your confidence along the way. It's important to celebrate every win—even the small ones. Every day, write down your wins, big and small, that relate to your dreams for the future. And give yourself credit for having a dream and a plan. Notice how far you've come.

In his book *Learning How to Avoid the Gap*, Dan Sullivan, the co-founder and creator of The Strategic Coach® program, talks about how many entrepreneurs focus on how far they have to go instead of looking at how far they've come. They focus on the gap between where they are now and where they want to be. That state of mind can hinder your growth, and you could end up negatively influencing others with that mindset.

Your future growth and progress are hindered or helped by the two different ways in which you can measure yourself: against the ideal, which puts you in what Sullivan calls "The Gap," or against your starting point, which puts you in "The Gain," appreciating all that you've accomplished.

When you're in The Gap, you feel as though you haven't accomplished anything at all. This is because even though you've moved forward, the ideal remains distant from you. The ideal is a moving target. It might even get bigger, leaving you worse off than where you started if you measure against it. You've also used up time and energy getting to where you are, so if you don't measure the progress, you'll feel like you've wasted that time and energy and have fallen even further behind.[60]

But if you turn around and measure your progress against where you started, then you're in The Gain and you'll experience a sense of having moved forward, of having achieved something, and you'll be motivated to continue on to your next stage of growth.

The problem with remaining in The Gap is that, from that perspective, there's nothing you can do about your distance from the ideal in that moment—it is what it is. The only thing you can do is make changes from that day forward to help get you where you need to go. There's no sense worrying about it, but maybe you need to change your plans. You are as far along as you are and should be. Your starting point is now.

---

60   Dan Sullivan, *Learning How to Avoid the Gap: The Skill of Lifetime Happiness* (Chicago: Strategic Coach, 2000).

INVEST IN YOURSELF

Investing in yourself is the best place to put your money. The investment into your personal growth or your future is really all that matters.

The people who are willing to invest in themselves and their future—who believe in themselves and their potential, regardless of what age or stage of life they're in—are the people who build great confidence. They are excited about the future.

For example, if you want to open a floral shop or a deli when you retire, start learning the trade and writing your business plan well in advance of your retirement. Or maybe you want to sail around the world when you retire. Imagine how exciting it will be as you master your sailing skills, talk with other people who've done the same thing, and plan your trip well in advance of your retirement.

Preparing for the future in advance helps people realize how much more they have to give in this world and that retirement doesn't have an end date.

Many people think retirement is the time when you slow down. We say the opposite: it's your time to speed up. With retirement, you finally have the time and the ability to invest in yourself. By the time most people retire, their kids are out of the house. It's often the first time they have put themselves first since before their children were born. Retirement is the time for you to focus on your needs and desires and answer only to yourself (and maybe your spouse).

MAKE DECISIONS BASED ON CHOICE, NOT FEAR

One of the rules of financial planning is to never make decisions based on unreliable emotions such as fear. Like we discussed in Chapter 7, people who pull out of the stock market at the first sign of a downturn typically regret it later. Investments should be a long-term proposition. Wait out the storm.

When people feel fearful, they are not in the best frame of mind for making decisions. Fear-based decisions can lead to mistakes, which can erode your savings as well as your confidence.

One way our Dream Architect™ process helps alleviate fear and builds confidence for our clients is by showing our clients what-if scenarios with possible outcomes based on certain parameters. We will show them what could happen in what they consider an absolute worst-case scenario. Often, that outcome is not nearly as bad as they had envisioned. When they can ask all their what-if questions and see the likely outcomes, it is a huge confidence builder.

Now, of course, no one has a crystal ball, and we cannot predict the future. But using historical trends, we can come up with fairly accurate assessments of which actions might result in which outcomes.

OPEN COMMUNICATION WITH YOUR ADVISOR BUILDS CONFIDENCE

When people come to us, one of the biggest sources of low confidence we see is a lack of communication with their previous financial advisors. It's not necessarily that they want to hear from their advisors all the time; rather, they want to be shown that regardless of what's coming up, things are likely to turn out okay. When the market is fluctuating wildly and they don't hear a word from their advisors, anxiety and worry often set in. When people see the markets going haywire, that's often when they make knee-jerk decisions and lose sight of their long-term goals because they don't have confidence that the future's going to be okay.

When people can enumerate potential outcomes and have their advisors walk them through various scenarios, it builds their confidence and calms their anxiety.

We mentioned in Chapter 2 that during the COVID-19 pandemic, those who have embraced The Dream

Architect™ process can be just as confident about their future as they were before the pandemic. But those who do not focus on the value of putting their dreams first may continue to be filled with uncertainty and worry. Knowledge builds confidence.

Confidence is critical to your ability to stay true to your plan. History tells us that when the market goes down—even significantly—it will eventually come back up:

After every decline in history, no matter how severe, investors tend to recover their losses, and markets begin to stabilize and see positive growth over the long run...Having the patience and discipline to stick with your investment strategy is vitally important in successfully managing any portfolio. And if you have a long-term investment strategy, you'll be far less likely to follow the panicking herd over the cliff...Instead of fear-based selling, use a bear market as an opportunity to buy more—accumulate shares at deep discounts in some cases and allow yourself to diversify, building a more stable base for when things eventually do turn around.[61]

---

61   Best, "3 Reasons Not to Sell after a Downturn."

DON'T COMPARE YOURSELF TO OTHERS

Another common habit that erodes people's confidence is comparing their situations to other people's situations. This is never a good idea. There will always be people who are better off than you are and some who are worse off than you are. Your situation is unique. Focus on what's important to you and your future. Avoid the temptation to compare yourself to others. No one needs to keep up with the Joneses. Chances are, what goes on behind the scenes may be very different than what you see at the surface.

Keep your eyes on your own paper and focus on what *your* definition of success is—not someone else's. As we mentioned in Chapter 3, don't let others "should" on you. Don't let people influence you in a negative way or throw you off course. You and your wealth advisor (and your spouse, if you have one) are a team. We have designed your plan according to your situation, dreams, and goals. It is customized to you. Chances are, other people—even family members—have no idea what all goes into your personally tailored financial plan. When you have a well-designed plan that is designed with your unique interests and future in mind, you will have enough confidence to tune other people out. They might mean well, but they are not helping when they don't know the details of your unique situation.

FOCUS ONLY ON WHAT YOU CAN CONTROL

The New York Stock Exchange was founded on May 17, 1792, when twenty-four stockbrokers signed the Buttonwood Agreement on Wall Street in New York City.[62]56 For more than 230 years, the markets have gone up and down. Can we control them? No. Can we time our buying and selling with the goal being to optimize every single return? Sometimes, if we're lucky.

The point is, we cannot control the markets. But it's amazing to see how many people try to do so. There is no use worrying about something you cannot control or predict. Focus on your portfolio's performance. Work with your advisor to make adjustments as needed.

Trying to time the market can cause you to head into The Gap Dan Sullivan described, focusing on how much further you have to go. When you guess wrong as you try to close that gap, it's easy to slip into a despairing victim mentality. This is why it's so important to focus only on what you can control.

So what *can* you control? Your mindset. Your decisions about what you want for your future. The actions and

---

62   "New York Stock Exchange (NYSE)," FXCM, December 11, 2014, https://www.fxcm.com/markets/insights/new-york-stock-exchange-nyse.

steps you take to save for that future. Your willingness to celebrate small wins to build your confidence. Your focus on how far you've come. Your recognition that it's pointless to waste time worrying about things you cannot control.

COLOR-CODING MAKES IT EASY
TO TRACK YOUR SUCCESS

We believe that evidence of success gives measure to a confident mind.

When you know your success ratio, built from an evidence-based report, it helps you make decisions faster and more confidently.

In our 2016 book, *Dare to Dream*, we described the color-coded system we use to show clients how they are progressing. This makes it easy for them to understand their situation at a glance.[63]

We make a visually clear presentation featuring red, yellow, and green, just like on a traffic signal.

- **Red** means we need to take some sort of action, something hasn't been done yet, or we need to

---

63   Sweet and Anderson, *Dare to Dream*, 77.

adjust an aspect of your financial plan, such as your spending. Red is a "stop" light—it means the decision you're thinking about making could have a negative impact on what you've said is important to you. When we see red, that signals we need to sit side by side and do a value realignment to make sure that your decisions reflect what you want most in your wealth plan.

- **Yellow** is a caution, indicating that we might need to adjust some details if the situation continues to move forward in the direction it has been going. We've all driven through a yellow light. If you have a yellow light in your plan, it doesn't mean you're not going to move ahead. It just means you need to take an extra look left and right a couple more times before you press your foot on the gas. Yellow means we might have to make some changes or tweaks to the plan to make your dream happen.

- **Green** means everything looks good for this aspect of your plan and you can move forward. Green means yep, go full steam ahead. The thing you want to do will not throw your plan off.

Our system evaluates how inflation and taxes can affect the rate of return for your investments and thus your spending goals. But we don't stop there; we take it one step further. We know you're not going to get the average rate of return every year and that inflation is not going to be the same every year, so we run the information through a thousand different iterations (called a Monte Carlo simulation). It assigns a probability our client will be able to meet all of the goals we entered into the system, given assumptions we specify. Although these projections regarding the likelihood of various investment outcomes are hypothetical and not guaranteed, they do give us an idea of your investments' future performance under various scenarios over time.

Using these color-coded, highly visual tools rather than a more conventional fifty- or hundred-page financial plan, it's much easier to show clients where they are in good shape and where they need to take actions. We do use those longer documents for clients who want all the details, but most clients don't want that level of detail. They want to know the time, not how the watch is made.

Plus, the powerful, vivid tools we use can be adjusted, affording an instant look at how a specific action will affect your plan. As we're sitting with you, you might look at the numbers we're presenting and ask, "Well, what if I purchase a winter home down South? And what if I pay for my three grandkids' college education?" We can show you, right then and there, how those actions will affect your plan and your probability of success in retiring at the age you have in mind.

Below is an example of a worksheet from a hypothetical client's retirement plan. The diagram shows the probability of a client's success given a specific set of parameters we entered into the system. The low percentage in the first circle indicates that the first scenario has a very low probability of success, requiring changes to be made.

After decreasing the amount by which the client's income would increase each year due to inflation, probability rose to 72 percent. Finally, by overhauling the client's plan, we were able to get it to a 96 percent success rate—in addition to the changes made to get it from 21 to 72 percent. And even though an overhaul sounds major, it doesn't have to be. It could be a combination of several seemingly minor items, such as selling a retirement home at an advanced age, as opposed to passing it on to heirs.

Some people are numbers-oriented, but others are not. We have found that the color system especially resonates with our clients who are not comfortable with numbers. For those people, we'll mention a number pertaining to their financial plan, and they'll ask, "What color is it?"

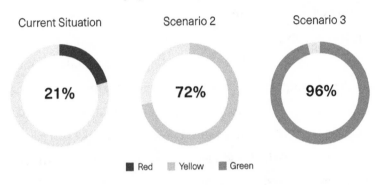

Probability of Success of a Specific Scenario

They understand that if it's green, they can do everything they want to do. They don't know the details, nor do they care, but they have the confidence that they can do what's important.

Seeing that green light is a confidence builder for people (and the yellow, to some extent).

LIVE TO YOUR FULLEST POTENTIAL
IN EVERY STAGE OF LIFE

In Chapter 2, we said the most important decision is what your true purpose is. To do that, you first have to acknowledge that you were put on this planet for a purpose.

In *Personality Isn't Permanent*, Dr. Benjamin P. Hardy shows that, well, your personality isn't permanent. For example, people often think that the line of work they've done for decades and the lifestyle they've had all that time define who they are forever. But that's not true. When you are encroaching on a major transition in your life, such as retirement, you probably need a different skillset than you've depended on during your career. This is a bigger issue for some people than it is for others. When people retire, many of them suddenly feel a disheartening void because the skills they have mastered for many years are no longer needed. That can cause a loss of identity and confusion about the role they will play in this new stage of life.

This is why it is important to know your purpose in life. When you look at yourself five, ten, or twenty years down the road, who do you want to be as an individual? Without knowing what your purpose on this planet is, how can you fulfill that life purpose moving forward? It would be a darn shame to just coast through life once you retire. Just because you retire doesn't mean you don't have a ton more to offer. Give yourself some self-love. Push yourself to fulfill your greatest potential in this new phase of life.

It will build your confidence to believe you truly are on this planet for a purpose and that your purpose will not be fulfilled until the day the good Lord takes you home. Nobody really likes to think about death. But remember, until your time is up, you will always have so much to give. We work hard to help people fully embrace that concept, especially when they are going through a major transition such as retirement.

PLANNING BUILDS CONFIDENCE

Confidence is something you can build; it's not something you're born with. Anybody can increase their level of confidence, as well as tangible results, by just planning.

In our experience, the people who struggle to set and articulate goals and dreams are the ones who lack confidence. We believe confidence is the key to accomplishment. If you know your purpose and what you have to contribute, you will have a clearer idea of what your plan for the future looks like, and that will build your confidence. Do the planning. If you don't, you aren't likely to reach your fullest potential.

We believe the people who are most confident are those who are able to clearly see and feel what is possible.

Sometimes people are embarrassed about the fact that they haven't taken the time to plan. You might not be confident in what you're doing today at this moment, but you can gain confidence by taking the right steps and going through the process to get to where you want to go. But you have to start as soon as you can—right now. No matter what your age is, whatever you do to improve your future will enhance your quality of life. If you don't ever start, you're never going to know what's possible.

Possibilities create confidence, and confidence improves your possibilities.

PLANNING GIVES YOU CONFIDENCE DURING LIFE TRANSITIONS

If you can look for and find the silver lining in all that happens in this life—good, bad, or indifferent—that's a reflection of your confidence when looking into the future.

We work with a lot of recently widowed spouses, mostly women. Of course, it is not positive when you lose your spouse. That's not a happy time for anybody. After suffering such a significant loss, people need to navigate the devastation, sadness, and grief. But imagine how much easier that entire process would be if the couple had sat down, years before, and planned for their future together with The Dream Architect™ process guiding them. If you delegate all the financial planning to your spouse and they pass away first, you are not likely to have much confidence about the future. You might not even know where you stand financially. So not only would you be facing extreme grief and loss; you would also need to master your finances. We want every widowed person we work with to be able to say, "I'm so glad I had you" versus "I wish I would have known."

When you have done all your planning, then you can be present in the moment you're in and feel what you need to feel versus having this open-ended concern about what might happen.

Confident people are more positive, and positive people are more confident. No matter what happens to them in life, they know they're going to be okay. This is why we believe there is no substitute for proper planning.

DO WHAT YOU REALLY LOVE

"If you don't know where you're going, you might end up someplace else."

—Yogi Berra

If you are a business owner, are you doing what you really love? Or are you focused only on that next level of success? When we are chasing success, it can be easy to put off doing what we love. We have mentioned this before, but we've seen people err on the side of saving too much and not having some of the experiences they could be enjoying right now. They are not confident that they're going to have enough in the future, so they deny themselves the joys of life now. They are basing their decisions on fear, not confidence.

If only they were to sit down with the right advisor, build a plan, and clarify what they want in the future, they would realize they could be doing so much more than they are. It is sad to see people working so hard and never taking a moment to dream about that big family vacation or gorgeous lake home or whatever else they would love to have in their lives.

Once you know what you want, you can be intentional about achieving it.

Life is too short to be uncertain about your future. As you move toward your dream life and what you want most out of your one go around the sun, spend your time with the people you love, doing the things you love. That will build your confidence. It will make it easier to see all the possibilities in your future.

YOUR TOOLBOX FOR
GAINING CONFIDENCE

In this chapter, we expressed the importance of focusing on one single outcome for the future and then devoting all your energy to that desired outcome. What is the one priority you want to focus on in retirement? This will look different for everyone. It could be family, traveling, building a business, flipping houses, moving overseas, or something else. Describe what your focus will be and why.[64]

_____

_____

_____

_____

_____

---

64   Note: For a little inspiration in finding your top priority, visit *www. mysweetfinancial.com* to access our Retirement Readiness Center.

CHAPTER 9

DREAM BIG AND THEN GO BIGGER AND BEYOND

"So many of our dreams at first seem impossible, then they seem improbable, and then, when we summon the will, they soon become inevitable."

—CHRISTOPHER REEVE

The quote above is by the courageous director, activist, and *Superman* actor Christopher Reeve. We think it is powerful, especially considering all that Reeve went through and how optimistic he remained, despite becoming paralyzed from the neck down in an equestrian accident at the age of forty-two.

After the accident, he continued to perform and was nominated for a Golden Globe for his work on a TV remake of *Rear Window*. He also directed several TV movies until his death at age fifty-two in 2004.

According to the Christopher & Dana Reeve Foundation website:

> The doctors took away any hope of improvement, assuring him that it was "impossible" to recover movement...The success story from the one who gave life to the most famous Superman on the big screen showed why, perhaps, as he would say, "the word *impossible* [is] no longer part of the scientific community's vocabulary."[65]

Reeve showed us that we need to dream big *all the time*, not just when your life is going great. The late actress, fashion icon, and philanthropist Audrey Hepburn said, "Nothing is impossible. The word itself says, 'I'm possible!'"

---

65 Patricia E. Correa, "A Single Centimeter, a Ruined Life: The Accident That Caused Christopher Reeve (Superman) to Go from a Star to Legend," Christopher & Dana Reeve Foundation, June 8, 2020, https://www. christopherreeve.org/blog/daily-dose/a-single-centimeter-a-ruined-life-the-accident-that-caused-christopher-reeve-superman-to-go-from-a-star-to-legend.

We want you to practice dreaming big and then push yourself to go bigger and beyond. Think of dreams so big that they set your heart on fire. Follow Napoleon Hill's advice: "Whatever the mind can conceive and believe, it can achieve."

Figure out what your heart desires most from life. Have fun brainstorming. Once you visualize it, you can make it happen.

We both can attest to the fact that when you put something in front of your mind that you want to achieve, even if it seems scary, your mind will find a way to bring that dream to fruition—as long as it's meaningful to you. If it's not that meaningful and it doesn't align with your values, then it will just go to the wayside. Your dream should be something that will give you the most fulfillment in life. Think even bigger than just a dream vacation with your family or traveling abroad.

So what does it mean to dream big? It means dreaming beyond your current capabilities. When you're dreaming big, you're forcing yourself to step into new abilities or a new role. A great way to remove the limitations from your mind is to ask yourself, "If time, money, and knowledge were not restrictions, what would I like to do? What are some capabilities that, up to this point, I wish I had?"

CONFIDENCE HELPS YOU DREAM BIG

Few people really allow themselves to dream big. One reason is because they lack confidence in themselves and their future. As we discussed in the previous chapter, planning for the future with the right advisor can increase your confidence, which will in turn fuel your ability to dream big.

Self-confidence is the foundation of your big dreams. But even though *self-confidence* is your belief in how good you are at something, it's not a *measure* of your actual skill.

Given that, why does it matter if you believe in yourself? According to Charlie Houpert, the author of *Charisma on Command* and the founder of a 2.7-million-subscriber YouTube channel of the same name, confidence doesn't just make you feel better; it also helps you take risks to make tangible improvements to your life.

To increase your confidence, Houpert recommends several strategies—among them, trying something new, exercising, and avoiding "impostor syndrome," a nasty mental bug that convinces you that your accomplishments don't really count and that you're going to be found out as a fraud. He says doubt can creep into our minds because it's easier for us to remember faults than it is to remember successes.[66]

---

66   Eric Ravenscraft, "Practical Ways to Improve Your Confidence (and...

To help you focus on your successes, make a habit of periodically writing down or reflecting on the things you've done well. It's easier to be confident in your abilities when you remember them. And again, celebrate even the small wins.

YOUR DREAMS ARE ALL ABOUT TOMORROW

"You have the power within. It's not your past that's going to define who you are, but it's what you believe about yourself; what you expect from yourself."

—Dr. Tererai Trent

When people get busy, they tend to accept whatever is in front of them. They are so focused on putting out today's "fires" that they don't have the time or energy to figure out what they wish for tomorrow. In addition, many people focus on their past mistakes instead of on their progress. But your dreams are all about *tomorrow*. You have the power to think beyond yesterday's mistakes and today's possibilities.

...Why You Should)," *The New York Times*, June 3, 2019, https://www.nytimes.com/2019/06/03/smarter-living/how-to-improve-self-confidence.html. Houpert's book is Charisma on Command: Inspire, Impress, and Energize Everyone You Meet (Scotts Valley, CA: CreateSpace, 2014).

Bryan was raised by a single mom and had no support from his dad. He had other loving family relationships that helped shape him. But Bryan could have easily gone into the victim mindset that says, *I can't dream big because I didn't have the same kind of life that other people had growing up.* Your past doesn't matter. What you do from this point forward is what matters.

Brittany was also raised by a single mom who did it all herself. Her mom struggled. There were times when Brittany would see her mom over her checkbook because she wasn't sure how she was going to make ends meet. She saw her mom endure the grind every day, working hard for long hours. She wasn't always able to be present for some of the activities that Brittany and her brother participated in. As a kid, sometimes that's hard to understand, but Brittany also thinks those experiences helped shape her. Her mom devoted herself to providing for her children, and for that, she is eternally grateful. Brittany also understands the major sacrifices her mom made in her life. Brittany never wants to endure the fear of being unable to provide for her family, and she knows that the only way she's going to have a different life is to make her ambitions a priority—to dream big.

If you have had painful experiences, use them to propel yourself out of limitation and motivate you to reach for the stars. Vow that you will never struggle again. Dream big, surround yourself with supportive people, and make your future much brighter than your past.

We encourage you to spend some time with an advisor who will help you think through that because the world is filled with immense opportunities and possibilities. But if we don't take the time to think about them, we will never experience them. And even if we do think about those big dreams, we must believe they can actually happen to us.

This entire book is about the importance of mindset in planning for the future. Your mindset is incredibly powerful. We can put numbers for your retirement on paper all day, but if you don't truly believe you can accomplish your dreams, they aren't likely to happen.

IN RETIREMENT, YOU FINALLY HAVE TIME

*"God allows us to experience the low points
of life in order to teach us lessons that
we could learn in no other way."*
—C. S. Lewis

Time is a precious commodity, and we can't get more of it. That means we must spend it wisely. The great news is that once you retire, you will finally have time to do all those things you wanted to do for years but never had time for. In our experience, what separates successful people from people who struggle financially is how they spend the time they're given every day.

When we're young, we are busy getting an education, starting careers, raising families, buying homes, building businesses, and often, just trying to master the act of juggling many responsibilities. But once you retire, you get to focus on yourself. That should be super exciting. Gone are the excuses that held you back from doing the things you love for all those years.

We can't bear to hear people say, "I'm too old to do those things now." Just the opposite is true—once you retire, it's finally time to *really* dream big and then dream bigger and beyond.

DREAM BIG WHILE NAVIGATING MAJOR LIFE TRANSITIONS

Major life transitions such as the death of a loved one, divorce, disability, losing a business—or even retiring and feeling unproductive—can certainly take the wind out of our sails. When we suffer crushing loss and grief, it can be challenging just to get through the next minute, much less to dream big for the future. We understand that major transitions can throw you off course and divert your focus from your future into the current moment. Those events can make it necessary to completely reshape what dreaming big means to you.

We have been there to support clients who have lost their spouse. They can barely force themselves to get out of bed. They are searching for what their new normal looks like. It's not realistic to expect them to focus on their dreams while they are in the middle of grief and mourning.

It is important to give yourself time to experience the grief, sadness, and sense of loss. But please understand that there is light at the other end of that tunnel. It might not look like it now and it might not even matter to you for a while, but eventually, you will regain your strength. Even when the bad stuff happens, there's possibility on the other side. It's going to look and feel different from what you knew before, but it's there.

In times of loss, it can be helpful to talk with someone you trust who has gone through a similar situation. When you are so close to the situation, it's difficult to see beyond it. Seeing how someone else got through grief and found hope again can help. We have seen quite a few of our clients who became widowed and thought they would never recover. But with the compassionate, kind, and patient support of close friends, they eventually found a path to a new future. For example, one of our clients had traveled extensively with her husband. When he passed away, she couldn't imagine traveling without him. But eventually, through encouragement, she began to book trips on her own and with groups, and she has found happiness again.

FIGURE OUT WHAT YOU *DON'T* WANT

Sometimes people have to decide what they *don't* want in order to decide what they *do* want.

Not many people know this because the first marriage was so short lived, but Brittany was divorced before she married her current husband. The person she was when she married the first time is not the person she is today. It was not a good relationship. She is a living testament to the fact that it is critical to surround yourself with positive people who support you.

Once Brittany decided to divorce her now-ex-husband, she had to rebuild her life and figure out what she wanted. She asked herself, *What the heck does my life look like, and who do I want to be? What's the next step, and what is the next big picture?*

Going through that transition was super hard. However, looking back now, Brittany considers it one of the biggest blessings and gifts in her life because it made her understand exactly what she *didn't* want, which then in turn helped her realize what she *did* want.

If you're willing to stop, figure out what you want your future to look like, commit to it, and take the steps to make it happen, you will end up in a much better place than where you are today.

It might not be easy, but if you put time, energy, and consistency into the effort, you will see great results. Follow the advice in this book, which is based on our personal experiences and observations, and you will be on the right path to new possibilities and reaching your highest potential. And ask for help; you don't have to do it all by yourself.

PUT SOME NUMBERS WITH YOUR DREAMS

Once you get an idea of what your dreams are, we can build your financial plan around them. In our initial Dream Architect™ workshop, we ask clients to list their dreams in order of priority, and then we assign a financial component to each one. That helps us determine what it will take for people to get where they want to go. Many times, people realize it doesn't cost a lot of money to realize their biggest dreams.

When you define your dream and begin assigning financial values to it, you will see that you have probably more than one option—more than one way to make your dream come true.

For example, let's say your dream is to have a house on the beach. The price tag, however, might seem way out of reach, especially when you consider the maintenance costs for the house. Well, you don't necessarily have to *purchase* a beach home to make that dream come true. What if you were to lease a nice beach house once a year or find a new one every summer on a vacation rental website?

If we dig deeper to find out *why* that beach house is important to you, we might discover that owning the house isn't what's important to you—your true priority is having your friends and extended family visit for fun summer vacations as a respite from their busy lives.

So if purchasing a beach home will eat too big a chunk from your savings, it doesn't mean your dream isn't possible. It means you will accomplish the same dream by taking a different path to achieve it.

WHAT ARE YOUR LIMITING BELIEFS?

One of our biggest societal problems is that when people feel strongly about something based on personal experiences, they think they're right. But often, we feel strongly about something simply because it's all we know. We've all had limited experiences that have shaped us up to this point, but that doesn't mean that every decision we've made was right.

Stephen Covey, author of *The 7 Habits of Highly Effective People*, talks a lot about the *abundance* mindset versus the *scarcity* mindset.

For example, people who grew up during the Great Depression often have a scarcity mindset. They scrimp and do without because they're terrified they won't have anything in the future. That's what they know, and they feel strongly about doing without some of life's pleasures to make sure they will have the necessities tomorrow. But that doesn't mean their approach is right or that it's ideal for everyone. We've said before that it's not a good idea to make decisions based on fear.

When someone has a mindset of abundance, they make choices based on what's possible. This is a much stronger position from which to build your future. Start by recognizing what your limiting beliefs are. That is the first step to letting yourself dream big.

The key is to challenge what you've always known, your existing beliefs. Think far beyond them and consider new possibilities. Keep doing that, and you will shape a new mentality and an abundance mindset. You will stretch your brain. If you stick with what you've always believed about yourself and your potential, you will not grow. By being open to possibilities, your success rate will increase immensely! It's okay if you've never attempted this dream before. It's okay if you know nothing about it. If it's meaningful to you and sets your heart on fire, set your intentions on it and plan the steps to make it happen.

TALK WITH SOMEONE WHO'S WHERE YOU WANT TO BE

Once you figure out what you really want, then find someone who has accomplished a goal like that. Reach out to them and ask to have a conversation. Expand your network. Earlier in this book, we talked about the importance of surrounding yourself with positive people who support you and champion your big dreams. While you are figuring out what your big dreams are, it's a perfect time to seek out mentors and people who share your dreams.

Ask for just ten minutes, and if the person you admire grants you that phone call, be prepared with questions. Ask that person how they accomplished that lofty goal, what lessons they learned along the way, and what recommendations they have that could benefit you.

It will energize you to speak with someone who has lived and breathed the dream you have in mind. It will help you eliminate your limiting beliefs and see that dream as a true possibility. Plus, once you establish that connection, you will have another positive, successful person in your corner, which will further help you reach your potential.

Why is this important? Because again, we don't know what we don't know. We aren't likely to learn something new and to broaden our options unless we seek out the perspectives of other people. If you don't know how to do something yourself, then you need a who to show you how.

We should always be seeking out opportunities to learn from successful big-thinking people. The more time we spend with them, the more doors will open for us, and the more possibilities will be made available to us. Plus, we have the chance to build deep, lasting relationships with some incredible people. Life can sometimes appear to be pretty negative, and it can be difficult to find people who believe in you. The people who look beyond all that negativity and naysaying are those who have amazing lives and who experience what's really important to them.

One book that Bryan particularly likes on the subject of mentorship is *Mentor to Millions* by *Shark Tank* host Kevin Harrington and serial entrepreneur Mark Timm. The book charts Timm's journey—from putting his work first and his family last to a whole new understanding of how work, life, and relationships can coexist and thrive together. With Harrington as his mentor, he learned how to win in every area of life, not just business.

BUSINESS OWNERS: DREAMING BIG
BENEFITS EVERYONE AROUND YOU

Business owners who began their business for a particular reason or who are carrying forth a family business sometimes get stuck in what they know. With technology advancing so quickly, the possibilities are endless for businesses to serve customers and clients in innovative ways.

If you are a business owner, to what extent have you examined your possibilities? Why not get everyone in your company involved in brainstorming? Ask everyone to come up with ideas for doing things differently and better. Offer rewards for those ideas you adopt. Not only will you strengthen your company's competitive position, but you'll also build camaraderie and buy-in, which will improve morale.

Our business is in a town of about ten thousand people, and people often tell us they can't believe some of the innovative things we're doing and the lives we've been able to impact through our work. From the creation of The Dream Architect™ to helping people design their version of what their ideal life looks like in retirement, we don't believe in limiting our capabilities due to our location. We choose to make it a point to dream big and then go bigger and beyond.

Brittany thinks this is a testament to Bryan and the culture he has established at Sweet Financial. Although some businesspeople in this moderately sized town may believe they're limited because of demographics, Bryan doesn't see that type of limitation.

When you dream big, it benefits everyone in your company. As a business owner, you are influencing the lives of many people—your employees, your customers, and their families. If you don't dream big with the products or services you offer and the way you offer them, you are doing a disservice to those people. Dream big, and you will enhance everyone's growth and well-being.

Dream big. See all that you can be with all you've been given.

When we talk about business owners who dream big, one particular client comes to mind. He grew up in a rural area and spent his life creating possibilities that have helped build a multibillion-dollar company. On top of all this, he is one of the most charitably inclined individuals we've ever encountered.

The client we are referencing knew what he wanted to build, figured out the steps to get there, and followed them consistently. Once he started to see results, that motivated him to dream even bigger. The more positive things he created, the bigger he dreamed, and the more positive things he built. It's a wonderful cycle. He truly mastered the art of surrounding himself with the right people and then getting out of their way.

GET STARTED, GAIN MOMENTUM, AND KEEP GOING

Building success is like driving a high-powered sports car. Even the fastest sports car in the world can't go from zero to one hundred miles per hour instantaneously. It goes from being in park to one mile per hour, and then two, and then twenty, and then thirty, and finally to one hundred. As it picks up speed, accelerating becomes easier. Once you gain momentum, your possibilities are endless.

That's true of our success, too. If we just get going in a specific direction with intent, passion, and a commitment to just one step of a bigger goal, we can build momentum and achieve what we want. Baby steps lead to bigger steps. You might be amazed at how much momentum you can pick up by committing to just the first step in your goal.

It's easy to feel overwhelmed by a "stretch" goal because it seems so far away from where we are now. Keep your eyes on the prize, but focus your daily attention on closing the gap just a little bit, doing one step at a time.

Think about how water boils. It starts out cold or at room temperature. As you apply heat, the water gets warmer and warmer. At 211°F, the water is super-hot, but it's not boiling yet. At 212°F, the water boils. Just 1° makes the difference between water that's boiling and water that's not. Once water begins boiling, it creates steam that can power motors and do other miraculous things.

Of course, your biggest dreams can't come to pass immediately; they take time, just like the boiling water. The earlier you begin planning, the more time you have to build toward your goals. The time to do these things is as soon as you possibly can. When you start planning early, not only are you benefiting your future; you're also serving as a role model for your kids, grandkids, and others around you who see how you are prioritizing your future and looking forward to your retirement with excitement.

The incremental steps toward the final outcome matter—a lot.

NEXT STEPS

We are giving you permission to believe in yourself and to dream big. You don't have to explain yourself or your reasons to anyone. Just make a commitment to yourself that you will design your happiest, most fulfilling life possible so you can make the most of your one go around the sun.

YOUR TOOLBOX FOR DREAMING BIG AND THEN GOING BIGGER AND BEYOND

For some, it is easy to dream big. For others, it can be a challenge to visualize all that is possible for the future. Visit *www.mysweetfinancial.com* to access our Retirement Readiness Center, where you will find tools and resources to help you uncover what you want your retirement to look like.

In the meantime, use the space below to write down some of the biggest dreams you have for your future. Remember, dreams mean different things to different people. What is important to you may not be what is important to others, and that is perfectly okay. This space is for *you*. It's for your dreams. It's to define all that is possible for your future.

DREAM BIG AND THEN GO BIGGER AND BEYOND

_____

_____

_____

_____

_____

_____

_____

CHAPTER 10

KNOW YOUR WORTH

"Hell on earth would be meeting the man
[or woman] you were supposed to be."

—KEITH CUNNINGHAM

S o many times, people ask the wrong question in retirement. They ask, "How much money do I need?" A better question to ask is, "What do I want to do with this life I've been given?"

Of course, the money is important—the numbers—but what's more important is that you focus on living your best possible life. Bryan Sweet says, "Concentrate on living richly, not on dying rich."

As we stressed in Chapter 9, we want you to dream big. You have worked hard, and you've navigated hardships and tough times. Don't limit your future potential. You are worth so much more than you realize. You are worth every ounce of effort you put into creating what you want most in life.

Many times, people don't realize what they are capable of, partly because nobody has taken the time or effort to tell them all the potential they see in them. As advisors, we view that as a critical role in helping people achieve their dreams for the future.

SELF-WORTH DRIVES ACTION AND HELPS BUILD YOUR CONFIDENCE

The dictionary defines self-worth as "the sense of one's own value or worth as a person." People sometimes use the term *self-worth* interchangeably with *self-esteem*, but some psychologists believe they aren't the same thing. They say self-worth should be less about measuring yourself based on external actions and more about valuing your *inherent worth as a person*. In other words, self-worth is about *who you are*, not about *what you do*.

Too many times, people base their self-worth on their careers or relationships. But when something in their career or relationship goes south, they suddenly consider themselves worthless and berate themselves. This is why it's important to assess your self-worth according to who you are, not what you do or the company you keep.

When you have a strong sense of self-worth, you will be more likely to give yourself permission to dream big and take bodacious steps to make those dreams come true. And that will build more confidence, which will propel you to take further positive actions. Dr. Wayne Dyer says, "Self-worth comes from one thing: thinking that you are worthy."

Regardless of how much wealth people have accumulated, that question—*How much money do I need?*—still comes up consistently. What they are really asking is, "Will I have enough money to do what I want in retirement?" But as we just stated, in our experience, we have found that the more important focus is what people want out of life. Then we can figure out how to help them allocate their resources to achieve those dreams. But you can't answer that better question until you really identify what you want most.

Throughout this book, we have encouraged you to master your mindset, pursue your biggest dreams, and focus on all the good life has to offer. Why? Because we know you are capable of so much. We believe fulfillment in life comes from being intentional about pursuing what you want. In this chapter, we explain why a strong sense of self-worth is a necessary foundation for making that happen.

LEARN TO FOCUS ON WHAT YOU WANT

What do you want?

Answering this question can be scary, especially if, until now, you've never put yourself first. It's scary because if you put an intention out there in the world, you'll feel committed to following through. But it's time to do so. Your biggest dreams might seem out of reach right now, but you are capable of achieving them. Just put your mind to it, and you will soon get used to the idea of accomplishing more than you ever dreamed.

In his book *Tiny Habits*, B. J. Fogg says that positive experiences reinforce good habits. We talked about momentum earlier, and we believe that when you start pursuing your dreams, the positive momentum you get from that forward motion will make you want to pursue those dreams even more.

It is incredibly rewarding for us to sit with clients and go through The Dream Architect™ process. People who have never asked themselves what they want start out somewhat reluctant to focus on what they want. It feels unnatural to them. But with their trusted advisors encouraging them, soon they begin brainstorming, and their faces—their entire beings—light up! They become excited as they talk about what they've always wanted to do. In many cases, those dreams lay dormant for decades as they took care of other people's needs. It's amazing to hear how good it feels for them to finally allow themselves to dream big.

Then, when they take those first baby steps toward fulfilling their dreams, it inspires them to keep going. The experience is so positive, they say, "What's next? What else can I do?" Suddenly, they are seeing the possibilities that were really there all along.

When you make progress, even incrementally, it makes you feel successful, which helps strengthen your sense of self-worth. Our Dream Architect™ process helps people feel successful as they strive for what matters most. This is a critical role, and we take it seriously. We believe you can live your biggest dreams much more easily if you have dream-focused advisors by your side, encouraging and guiding you.

When people attempt something new, it can be uncomfortable for them, and they are likely to make mistakes as they try to master the new skill. It can make them feel clumsy, stupid, or unsuccessful, and as a result, they often give up. We have helped hundreds of people retire, and we can help you get past those early feelings of discomfort and unfamiliarity.

As your trusted advisors, we will remind you that you bring incredible value to this world, and we will encourage you when doubts and fears clamor for your attention. We want you to look far beyond what life has presented to you so far. You don't know what you don't know, and we can help you figure it all out.

You don't have to know how if you know who. We look forward to being your who on your journey to and through retirement.

STRATEGIES FOR SCARY TIMES

In his "'Scary Times' Success Manual," Dan Sullivan, Strategic Coach®, helps people discover how a short-term negative experience can lead to permanent growth. The article serves as a how-to guide for business owners and other leaders who are responsible for guiding others through scary times.

Sullivan describes ten strategies for transforming the negative into a positive. For example, one strategy is "Forget about your losses and focus on your opportunities." Another one is "Forget about what's missing; focus on what's available." And a third one is "Forget about your commodity and focus on your relationships." That third principle is certainly applicable to business owners, and it is a mantra we live by at Sweet Financial. In our experience, the people who have successful, fulfilled retirements are not focused on investment management—the commodity. They are focused on finding partners who can help them make their wealth work for them so they can achieve everything their hearts desire.[67]

If you find yourself focusing on the negative aspects of a situation instead of the positive, catch yourself doing it early on and change your focus. It takes practice, but you can do it. A positive mindset is especially important during scary times like the COVID-19 pandemic.

DISCOVER WHAT YOU CAN BE

"Make the most of yourself by fanning the tiny, inner sparks of possibility into flames of achievement."

—Golda Meir

Going through the process of self-discovery, many people find it difficult to focus on the future. They tend to—almost by habit, it seems—bring up their past failures and ruminate on them. We remind them that the future is all

---

[67] Dan Sullivan, "'Scary Times' Success Manual: How to Be a Leader When Times Get Tough," *The Multiplier Mindset Blog*, Strategic Coach, accessed February 10, 2022, https://resources.strategiccoach.com/the-multiplier-mindset-blog/scary-times-success-manual-how-to-be-a-leader-when-times-get-tough.

there is. The past is done, and the present will soon be the past, so the only place you can create value or something better is in the future.

Don't worry about things that haven't been perfect up to this point because you can't do anything about them. Focus on where you will go from here. Rather than focusing on who you were, focus on who you can be.

If you've never had a mindset of focusing on the best the future has to offer, you can begin right this minute to adopt that mindset. We do not believe in the tired adage, "You can't teach an old dog new tricks." People have proven throughout history, time and time again, that it's possible to do amazing things at any point in life, at any age.

To help get yourself in the habit of thinking about the future and about what's important to you, again, we encourage you to get a copy of our book *Imagine. Act. Inspire.* As we mentioned, it's a daily journal for you to fill out. We mentioned this journal earlier—each day provides a positive quote for you to practice naming your gratitudes and to-do lists.

WHAT IF YOU'RE JUST NOT A "FUTURE THINKER"?

Now, we have been stressing heavily that it's best to focus on the future and not get stuck in the past. We do believe that, but we also understand that focusing on the future is difficult for some people.

We both love looking forward to the future and getting excited about what will come next. But we also know people who find it challenging to envision what's happening down the road or to ponder the possibilities that could potentially come about. These people find it more comfortable to focus on the present. It is important to honor that approach. If you're not a future thinker, it's okay. As financial planners, sometimes we have to be intentional about being present because we become *too* future focused. We realize that some of the concepts we've talked about in this book might feel a little overwhelming to people who are not future focused.

If that is your experience, then all you have to do is look at where you are right now in your life and identify the things that really matter to you in this moment. Ask yourself, *To what extent am I pursuing those things that make me really happy?* If there is a big gap between what you're doing now and what you'd like to be doing, you can identify the steps you need to take to close that gap.

For example, many of our clients realize as they near retirement that they have not spent enough quality time with the people they love. Many of them also realize that they don't like cold winters, so they plan ways to spend time with their grandkids in warmer climates during the winter. If that is something that is important to you and would make you happy, start by identifying what that looks like. Block out time on your calendar and make a commitment to spending quality time with your favorite people.

START SMALL

Philanthropy is another priority for many of our clients. They really want to make a difference in the world through supporting organizations they believe in, but they've never figured out how to make that happen. We encourage them first to identify those organizations they really believe in. Then they can start small with their charitable endeavors—maybe contact someone on the organization's board and ask how they can contribute. Maybe spend time volunteering and getting to know what the organization needs most.

Without a plan, people can end up just spinning their wheels and not taking any action. We have seen wealthy entrepreneurs who get so hung up on trying to find the perfect charity aligned with their values that they never settle on one organization to help. This is another reason why it's a good idea to start out small: you might discover down the road that an organization you thought was ideal for you actually isn't. If that happens and you started out small instead of donating a hefty sum of money, then you have reserves to explore other organizations that are better suited. Once you find the charity that speaks to your heart and aligns with your values, you can make bigger contributions of time, money, and effort.

The point here is that the simple act of contributing to something that is bigger than yourself can be a catalyst for helping you live a more enriched and fulfilled life. We have been so fortunate over the years to work with clients who are true givers by nature—who believe that their wealth is not just their own but something they can use to spread light to others.

When we look at the importance of dreaming big, impact and legacy are two things that we hear most frequently from our clients. Again, we encourage you to define your dream life and do whatever it takes to help you achieve it.

NEXT STEPS

We want to end this chapter, and this book, by stressing how important it is to view retirement as your new beginning. We want you to look forward to retirement so you can accomplish all those things that "fill your cup" and make you feel happy and fulfilled. You have so much to give to the world. Believe in yourself, surround yourself with positive people who believe in you, and set your intentions on your biggest possible dreams. As you take that journey, we hope you will call on us to be your whos— your advisors who will guide you every step of the way.

If you have not done as much as you would like about planning for your future because you didn't know how to get started or who to consult, then we hope you will contact us. We know retirement can seem overwhelming. But the great news is this: all you have to do is take small steps at first, and we will guide you along the way.

We hope you have found at least one, and perhaps many, tips in this book that will help you think differently. We hope you understand now that your mindset about retirement is just as important as the numbers are.

We wish you the most amazing future—you can have one!

YOUR TOOLBOX FOR
KNOWING YOUR WORTH

1. Visit *www.mysweetfinancial.com* and download the Appreciate Your Worth tool found in our

Retirement Readiness Center. Work through this to uncover where you shine and how you can use your abilities to impact your future.

2. How strong is your sense of self-worth? If it isn't that strong, what do you think are some reasons for this? If you do have a strong self-worth, how do you think you developed it?

_____

_____

_____

_____

3. Imagine that it's three years in the future and you are looking back on the past three years. What needs to have happened during that time for you to feel good about your progress?

_____

_____

_____

_____

ABOUT THE AUTHORS

Brittany Anderson is the President of a top wealth planning firm, an influential speaker, and author. She has spoken on stages across the US, helping people to pursue futures they didn't know were possible. Her insights have been featured in national media outlets such as *HuffPost* and *Women Inc.*

Bryan Sweet has been repeatedly recognized by multiple industry publications as one of the top financial advisors in the US, including the *Forbes* Best-in-State Wealth Advisors, the Inc. Top 5000 list of fastest-growing companies, the Financial Times 400, *Research* magazine's Advisor Hall of Fame, and more.

Together, they help their clients realize their greatest dreams for life and retirement at *sweetfinancial.com.*

Sweet Financial
PARTNERS